The Industry of
Marrying Europeans

T0349481

Vũ Trọng Phụng
Thúy Tranviet, translator
introduction by Thúy Tranviet

The Industry of Marrying Europeans

SOUTHEAST ASIA PROGRAM PUBLICATIONS
Southeast Asia Program
Cornell University
Ithaca, New York
2006

Cornell Southeast Asia Program Publications
640 Stewart Avenue, Ithaca, NY 14850-3857

Southeast Asia Program Series No. 22

Printed in the United States of America

ISBN-13: 978-0-877271-70-3 hc / ISBN-10: 0-877271-70-4 hc
ISBN-13: 978-0-877271-40-6 pb / ISBN-10: 0-877271-40-2 pb

Cover Design: Marie Tischler

CONTENTS

ACKNOWLEDGMENTS

This small project started many years ago, back in my school days at Ann Arbor, in fact. Over the years many people have contributed to making it what it is today. Thanks to Nancy Florida and John K. Whitmore, who offered valuable comments on early drafts—they will always be my mentors. Although small, this book speaks in many languages. I'm grateful to Nguyễn Hữu Luận and Ngô Như Bình, who shed light into the nuances of our mother tongue. Thanks to Sylvie Doutriaux, Marc Brunelle, and Christophe Robert, a native French speaker who has taken to speaking pidgin French ever since he came aboard. On the English end, I am most indebted to my friend and colleague Keith W. Taylor, who literally brought this project back to life. I am sure he is as relieved as I am that it is finally finished. For moral support, I am grateful to my family and dearest friends—they are the backbone of my being. Last but not least, I am fortunate to have worked with two fine editors. Michael Wakoff made perceptive comments and spent endless hours on the translation. The capable, cool, and collected Deborah Homsher made everything look good with her keen insights and marvelous editing skills. All errors are mine.

Thúy Tranviet
Ithaca, NY
October, 2005

VŨ TRỌNG PHỤNG'S
THE INDUSTRY OF MARRYING EUROPEANS:
A SATIRICAL NARRATIVE

Thúy Tranviet

Romance and adventure inspire many people to write. The combination of the two elements makes an interesting topic, as the elements themselves are often the key that captivates the general reading public's appetite for sensation and thrills. Of many books that have been written about the French Foreign Legion, some offer historical background and glimpses of France's fighting forces, and many are personal memoirs from the members of the mercenary corps. In many of the so-called memoirs, legionnaire soldiers have taken the trouble to explain the personal motivation that led them to join the forces. Their reasons ranged from an ambition to become professional soldiers to a desire to feel loyalty to an institution other than their own countries, from which they were seeking refuge. Some claimed they were looking for adventure. Many cited romance as a motivation; the notion of being with someone of a different race in an exotic land is considered romantic. This romance element has been responsible for the popular belief that many of these memoirs seem to be more fiction than factual, or at least contain a mixture of both. On the other hand, very few authors—writers of fiction or non-fiction—have written about the native women with whom these legionnaires might have carried on a romantic courtship. Vũ Trọng Phụng's *Kỹ Nghệ Lấy Tây* (The Industry of Marrying Europeans) is a piece of reportage about the Vietnamese women who married European Legionnaire soldiers in French Indochina.

Vũ Trọng Phụng wrote this documentary narrative in 1934, after a few days of interviewing European legionnaires and Vietnamese women in Thị Cầu, a village in Bắc Ninh, a town thirty-five kilometers north of present-day Hanoi. The author claimed that he began his journey out of curiosity, because of a statement made by one of these women in a courtroom, that her "occupation" was marrying Europeans. While searching for such an "industry," he was also curious about the motivations behind the unions of the Vietnamese women and the Europeans. He wondered about the significance of romance in these liaisons, asking whether or not the cross-cultural "activity" among these men and women was indeed an industry. From his findings, Phụng created this reportage, which is more than a report, but not quite a novel, and far from a memoir. This work is a satire.

Born in Hanoi in 1912, Vũ Trọng Phụng died of tuberculosis in October 1939, a week shy of his twenty-seventh birthday. He came from a humble background: he was born in poverty, lived poorly, and died in poverty. Phụng's inherited poverty was one factor that greatly shaped his writing. His father, a blacksmith, died of tuberculosis when Phụng was only seven months old, and in a small one-room residence on Hàng Bạc Street, in the center of the old quarter of Hanoi, Vũ Trọng Phụng grew up with his grandmother, his mother, and two older sisters. The two sisters later went to Đáp Cầu, a nearby town, to work as live-in maids. Deprived of education due to financial difficulties (he only finished primary school), Phụng had to go to work early to support his family. At sixteen, he worked as a clerk in a French publishing house, where he eventually got fired, reportedly because he was discovered typing stories on the job. He later found work in other newspaper companies and turned to writing as his main source of income. It has been observed that he was a "civil servant writer" (*nhà văn công chức*) because whereas his contemporaries came from more affluent backgrounds, Phụng depended on his writings for his livelihood. Ironically, it has also been said that had he not been so poor, perhaps he would not have written as much as he did, in which case modern Vietnamese literature would have been robbed of some of its most important works.

Given the short span of his writing career, the extent and legacy of his works was anything but modest. When he died at the age of twenty-seven, Phụng left behind no less than eight completed novels, seven long works of reportage, six plays, a score of short stories, and several translations, all of which were set in the contemporary period of the French occupation of Indochina. A tireless writer, in 1936 alone he wrote no less than three long novels and one piece of reportage. *Số Đỏ* (Lucky destiny),[1] his most celebrated novel, came out that year. Over the years, there have been hundreds of articles written analyzing and debating issues raised by this novel, and in 1990 a six-hour film was produced based on the novel. This momentous work tells the story of a man who is transformed from being dirt-poor to rich, from a vagabond to a respected citizen, in a class-differentiated society that is so corrupt and caught up with Westernization that it does not know the difference between what it is real and what is not. With its witty prose, funny scenarios, and unforgettable characters, the novel acts as a looking glass into the Vietnamese society of the author's time.

Vũ Trọng Phụng was obsessed with topics that were considered "taboo" or "deviant" in 1930s society, and he openly depicted the culture's unwanted elements, deviants, and the people some might call "lowlifes." In responding to the injustices that the society heaped on less fortunate individuals like himself and his characters, he used his pen and his sense of humor as weapons. He wrote candidly about the lives of opium addicts, gamblers, cheaters, rapists, and prodigal sons and daughters, as well as their corrupted parents. Some of his best known works of reportage are centered on the lives of household servants and their masters, and of prostitutes and

---

[1] The translation of *Số Đỏ* is available under the title *Dumb Luck*, translated by Nguyen Nguyet Cam and Peter Zinoman (Ann Arbor, MI: The University of Michigan Press, 2002).

their madams. Phụng has been classified as a "social realist" writer, even though many Vietnamese literary critics would hesitate to consider him in the same school as Nguyễn Công Hoan, Nam Cao, or Ngô T t Tố. In the words of Tố Hữu, a socialist poet: "Vũ Trọng Phụng did not write for the Revolution, but the Revolution thanked Vũ Trọng Phụng."[2] What makes Phụng different from his contemporaries is that he claimed that he did not write fiction, but true stories. In fact, he did both.

The Industry of Marrying Europeans is a documentary narrative that embodies a great deal of truth, but not without a blend of fiction. Perhaps no other Vietnamese writer at that time was more renowned than Phụng for writing reportage, as indicated by the popular title he earned—"king of reportage," or *ông vua phóng sự* (*ông vua*, king; *phóng sự*, reportage). In Vietnamese, the word "reportage," or the term *phóng sự*, can be broken down so that it yields further meanings; *phóng* means to "write after a model," but it can also suggest "to enlarge" or "to aggrandize," while *sự* means "event." In other words, the phrase *phóng sự* implies exaggeration and therefore suggests much more than an objective account recorded by a reporter. Hence, while retaining elements of the truth, a *phóng sự* writer has the freedom to exaggerate the event in order to make the story more interesting. Vũ Trọng Phụng had always been motivated by the truth, as he had often said in his writings. However, cursed by "inherited" poverty, he was very cynical about life in the 1930s. The author intuitively turned to fiction and humor because they allowed him the freedom to carve a haven for both his own comic relief and an imaginary salvation. If the truth-seeking aspect in his work made Vũ Trọng Phụng a reporter, his ability to fictionalize the truth made him a writer. He was known for writing reportage that reads like a novel and for writing novels that read like reportage. Phụng's acute and distinctive imagination and his ability to convey dramatic elements in his reportage and in his portrayal of fictional characters and situations are both realistic and uncanny. In his interview with Mrs. Kiểm Lâm, the conversation starts out normally between (the reporter) and his subject:

> "I wouldn't think all of them are like that," I said.
> "Well, some of them are quite kind. But that seems to be my fate; I seem to run into the good-for-nothing types. What can I do? That soldier was a German. In his country, he was a hit man and left it to come here. Don't you think we are brave, sleeping with murderers? He has a nice face, but his soul is evil."
> Her voice was getting softer and her head was moving ... toward me.

Then Phụng seems to drift out of the interview into this imaginary event that is presented as if it happened between the poor Mrs. Kiểm Lâm and her "husband":

> *One night, a legionnaire turned up the wick of the oil lamp. He looked at his wife's face carefully and asked:*
> *"I am very good looking, aren't I?" [says he]*
> *"Yes, very handsome." [replies she]*
> *"But, I have killed someone." [he]*

---

[2] Nguyễn Đăng Mạnh, "Introduction," in *Vũ Trọng Phụng: Selected Works* (Hanoi: Văn Học Publishing, 1987).

> *"Don't be a liar."* [she]
> *"Liar? Don't you want to know my crime?"* [he]
>   *Then the legionnaire gritted his teeth and stared at his wife. Under the light, his handsome face had changed into a scary monster. Madame Kiểm Lâm was terrified; she screamed and turned her head to the wall ...*

And then Phụng (the reporter) goes back to his interview:

> "Can you imagine someone who is so good looking that he could make you fall in love with him in one instant, but is terrifying to you the next? I have seen such a face ... two faces, as a matter of fact!"

In his reportage, Phụng often uses this tactic of shifting back and forth between non-fictional reporting and fictional invention to intensify the parody of the situation. The combination of Vũ Trọng Phụng's many aspects—the fiction writer and the documentary recorder, the social commentator, the cynic, the humorist, the multifaceted persona—produced a collection of some of the best and possibly most outlandish works in modern Vietnamese literature.

Although Vũ Trọng Phụng was known to write about the social issues of the 1930s, his interests and talents extended beyond them. His successes were due to his keen observation of society and his dry, witty sense of humor. That wit is exemplified in Phụng's intentional use of the word *kỹ nghệ* (industry) to imply that the marriages of the local Annamite women and the European men were mechanical and businesslike matters. The term "industry" in Vietnamese encompasses places, like factories, that employ many workers. As a hired laborer, a man or woman works for a price, and the length of one's employment depends implicitly on the monetary value of one's service. Marriage is supposed to be a happy occasion, a celebration of joy, and the ultimate test of love and respect; marriage is not usually considered to be an occupation, let alone an industry. The title—or, to be more precise, the contradiction in the title—suggests that the author's intent was, in fact, to write satire.

There are many definitions of satire; the American Heritage dictionary defines it as "an artistic work in which human vice or folly is attacked through irony, derision, or wit." Leonard Feinberg sums it up: "Satire is a playfully critical distortion of the familiar."[3] This essay will argue that Phụng employed satire as an instrument of exaggeration with the intent of criticizing, while sustaining a comic tone. Satirical works generally use both criticism and humor as elements, and Phụng's works contain both, although often it is easier to recognize only one and not the other.

Vũ Trọng Phụng claimed to seek the truth, but in fact the truth was looking for him. Even though the author said that he set out to find whether there was indeed an "industry" of marrying Europeans, he was not at all interested in the history of this "occupation," as it had always been considered the oldest occupation in the world, so that any concern with its history would not be unnecessary. His report on this industry is delivered by a first-person male narrator and deals mostly with the encounters between this narrator and Vietnamese women, their European

---

[3] Leonard Feinberg, *Introduction to Satire* (Ames, IA: The Iowa State University Press, 1967), p. 19.

"husbands," and their offspring, the Eurasian "products" of these unions. The narrative suggests that Phụng was certainly curious about the interracial relationships between the local Annamite women and European men, but he was especially interested in the predicament of the Eurasian children, the offspring of these people. Recognizing the social prejudices prevalent at the time, which discriminated against mixed-blood children, depriving them of proper education and denying them a cultural identity, Vũ Trọng Phụng was curious to see how this new socio-cultural space would fit within traditional society. However, he was not calling for East-West assimilation or the harmonious cross-cultural transformation of Indochina at that time. It was the irony of the situation that most interested Vũ Trọng Phụng.

As in any work of investigative journalism, the reporter would naturally use the first-person voice to record and narrate the dialogues that took place between him and his characters. The narratives in this work are written from the first-person point of view, and the reportage reads rather like a play because it contains dialogues and scenes that invite the audience's reactions. Not only did Phụng go to great lengths to reconstruct, invent, and imagine the dialogues and lives of his informants, he was also able to transform himself throughout the narrative, shifting in and out of the text, and to successfully carry on dialogues with his readers as well. Literary critic Nguyễn Đăng Mạnh suggests that Phụng created another character that "is not him but very much like him."[4] The character "I" in *The Industry of Marrying Europeans* is not only the protagonist of the story, but also the most important character, because he bridges the roles of two essential characters—Vũ Trọng Phụng the reporter and Vũ Trọng Phụng the writer. Perhaps the question that should be examined concerns the "voices" or the "dialogues" of these first-person narratives: to whom is this person talking? to the readers or the subjects investigated or interviewed?

The character "I" is the voice of Phụng's alter ego; it gives him the social space that enables him to act as a liaison between his other characters or informants and his readers. This is not the character "I" that Greg Lockhart refers to in his discussion of the first-person narratives from the 1930s.[5] Similarly, it is not the same "I" that Tam Lang used in his reportage, *Tôi Kéo Xe* (I pulled the rickshaw).[6] Both Tam Lang and Vũ Trọng Phụng wrote first-person narratives, but Tam Lang's "I" serves as a "social bridge," a means to make him equal with other rickshaw coolies. One might also argue that, in such cases, a first-person narrator serves as a tool for investigative journalists who wish to take on the roles of their subjects, to go "undercover" in order to immerse themselves in the subcultures they were sent to investigate. Phụng, on the other hand, manipulates the "I" in this work so that it serves many roles: in some places the pronoun represents the writer himself talking to his readers, but it also stands for a fictional character, his persona, which he created to play himself. Only by inventing the character "I" could Phụng be comfortable with his informants as well as with his readers.

Coming from a poor background and a skeptic by nature, Phụng was known to mingle with social rejects; his novels are mostly centered around the themes of prostitution in *The Industry of Marrying Europeans*, *Làm Đĩ* (Prostitution), and *Lục Xì*

---

[4] Nguyễn Đăng Mạnh, "Introduction."

[5] Greg Lockhart and Monique Lockhart, trans., *The Light of the Capital: Three Modern Vietnamese Classics* (Kuala Lumpur and New York: Oxford University Press, 1996), pp. 6–13.

[6] Tâm Lang, *Tôi Kéo Xe* (Los Amitos, CA: Xuân Thu, 1988).

(The VD clinic); thievery and corruption in *Giông Tố* (The storm), *Số Đỏ* (Lucky destiny), *Cạm Bẫy Người* (How to trap people), and *Cơm Thầy Cơm Cô* (Household servants); and opium addiction in *Giông Tố*, and so forth. However the author himself was reportedly a devoted son and a good husband who had no experience drinking or gambling. He was quiet and reserved and was extremely shy when interacting with women. Even after he had become well-known, he still dressed modestly, most of the time in traditional Vietnamese clothing.

The invention of the character "I" is a strategy that provided the author with a voice to fill the gap between the factual reporter and the inventive writer. When, in this work, he constantly asks readers to "try to understand," Vũ Trọng Phụng places himself on the same level as his readers. Through his writing, he was also trying to understand life's ridiculousness and ironies. This effort is apparent in the conversation between our narrator and "the camel," an old legionnaire, who had just got "married" to Mrs. Kiểm Lâm.

> I had to "roll my tongue seven times" before I could answer:
> "If you say that, then in my country since the beginning of time, all marriages are business transactions. As you probably already know, the majority of the people in my country still follow the old customs. There aren't many people who are able to marry the ones they love. It never happens in my society that a young couple is able to discuss their affairs freely with one another. So receiving offerings from a man is no different than a business transaction. The ten piastres that you gave her, according to our marriage customs, I would consider that as a form of a dowry from the groom's family. That's all. Life is very simple. Please don't worry that I laugh at you because if I did so, I would have to laugh at my country first."

In this passage, the narrator, or perhaps Phụng himself, questions the social condemnation of prostitutes by arguing that a one-time encounter with a prostitute is not actually much different from sex with a lifelong partner or wife. The speaker contends that since voluntary marriages for love are rare occurrences in Vietnam, marrying a good girl is like getting a life-term prostitute. And if that were true, it could be argued that this speaker questions the conventional condemnation of prostitution with sound logic. This passage is presented as a conversation between Phụng and one of the legion's soldiers, but it could also be interpreted as Phụng, the author, talking to his readers. By speaking directly to the readers, he is able to explain and justify his statements, establish a bond of camaraderie, and even win their confidence. At first glance, the writer seems to be unsympathetic towards these women who engage in marriage as an industry because he ridicules them for being unrefined or uncivilized or even crude, yet a closer analysis reveals that the author is mocking other aspects of Vietnamese culture and questioning traditional customs, including the institution of marriage.

It seems that Phụng's "I" consistently fought with what was considered "right" or "proper" by both society's and his own standards. As the narrative and dialogues weave in and out of each other, Phụng increasingly finds comfort in his adoption of a new persona. The character "I" is a strategy that allows him to be, or "to take on a role" as, a reporter "who goes here and there and reports whatever is interesting." By adopting this persona, he is able to share some of his thoughts with his subjects and divulge others to his readers, thereby concealing his own feelings. In some cases, the first-person narrator describes troubling situations objectively in a way that would have been impossible for the author if he were expressing his own opinions and views of these events; the author's and narrator's points of view diverge in these passages, a technique that gives the author another voice to use for his satire or to make fun of himself.

> Suzanne's explanation gave me a new perspective on the two views of beauty. But I still wanted to know how did those ugly-as-a-ghost dames manage to get married? And speaking of ugliness, Madame Ách was definitely in that category. So, then, how am I going to ask her? I went in circles:
> "Perhaps to the Westerners, beauty isn't the only thing that matters. Some of them probably have a high regard for personality, and they probably want to have a decent, virtuous wife. That must be the reason then, so those ladies who are not exactly beauty queens wouldn't do so badly after all ... "
> Suzanne turned out to be better than I was: She was honest.

Nearly every episode in *The Industry of Marrying Europeans* is touched by both comedy and tragedy. This is a work where the plot is set so that both Phụng the writer and Phụng the reporter can be in the story and sharing the stage together. When there is a scene that requires the reporter to speak, then the writer stands aside observing and narrating. And in some of the scenes, the reporter joins the author and the audience.

> To be honest, I [*writer*] was being quite ... clever. I [*reporter*] continued:
> "I [*reporter*] have read quite a bit about marriages, and I [*reporter*] feel bitterly torn. For example, this Western philosopher, well, unfortunately, I [*both*] can't recall his name (well, how could I [*writer*] really since I [*writer*] am making this up?).

Humor can be defined as the ability to recognize and to convey the comical aspect inherent in a situation. When a situation or the behavior of individuals engaged in it proved to be unconventional from the author's perspective, they were often parodied or satirized, and the author's feelings toward these concerns were frequently manifested through humor. This exemplifies the fundamental mechanics of satire, as the author recognizes the absurdity of the situation and chooses to attack by deploying a comic remark—or, as in many of Phụng's dialogues, silence, as manifested in the conversation between Phụng and one of the legionnaires, Dimitov:

> "Why did you rape her in the first place?" I asked.
> "Because when she was selling bananas, she behaved so ... well, like a whore."
> ...
> I looked at another fellow smoker. He answered me by shaking his head. One never understands the complicated love affairs of the legionnaires. As for the person who had just left, my Dear Readers, please remember that once upon a time Dimitov was a "hero."

In the ten years of his writing career, Vũ Trọng Phụng wrote several plays, one of them entitled *Cái chết bí mật của người trúng số độc đắc* (The mysterious death of the lottery winner).[7] This short play is about a particular young man who died mysteriously the day after he won the grand prize in the state lottery. The play focuses on the investigation and trial surrounding his death. As the trial proceeds, the court seems not to be able to reach a verdict about whether or not foul play had taken place. In the end, the court declares that the lottery winner died by suicide and explains the reasoning behind this judgment by announcing that the young man was a narcissist, who chose not to live because he could no longer face his own good looks. Imagine what the courtroom was like when the verdict was announced: the essence of the verdict itself was not funny, yet because of its nonsensical text, it was a mockery, which could be exposed only through humor. The play was intended to be light and humorous, but it did not conceal the fact that Phụng had very little confidence in the court system.

Just as Phụng followed the dark road that led him to Thị Cầu, where most of the women he interviewed lived, his narratives take us to this newly discovered cross-cultural society. Most of the activities and dialogues among the dames in the Thị Cầu area, and between the author and the dames, were recorded in *quốc ngữ*, the Vietnamese romanized script.[8] Besides the standard Vietnamese language, in the course of his research Phụng also recorded two other "languages." The author used French to record conversations among the French or between the elite Vietnamese and the French. These types of conversations would usually occur in government workplaces, such as court rooms, police stations, and so forth. The third language is a Vietnamese transliteration of French. By using the *quốc ngữ* writing system based on Vietnamese phonetics, the author recorded the sounds of a "kind-of-French language." To the French-educated Vietnamese, this "kind-of-French language" was known as *Tây bồi* (where *Tây* means "Western" or "French" and *bồi* is probably derived from the English word "boy" for *garçon* [waiter or servant]). *Tây bồi* is a mishmash of French and Vietnamese, mostly spoken by lower-class Vietnamese. It can be called "pidgin French" because the speakers have had little or no formal education in French, but have usually picked up this language by working with (or marrying) the Europeans.[9] Since proper French grammar is ignored in *Tây bồi*, and the pronunciation is very heavily accented with Vietnamese, this "kind-of-French language," or French-based pidgin, can be incomprehensible to speakers of (good or correct) French who are not familiar with it or are not Vietnamese speakers. However, people can certainly learn these sounds and use them to communicate effectively with each other. The Vietnamese "dames" and their European "husbands" (many of whom were non-native French speakers in the French Foreign

---

[7] Vũ Trọng Phụng, "Cái chết bí mật của người trúng số độc đắc" [The mysterious death of the lottery winner], in *Vũ Trọng Phụng: Selected Short Stories*, ed. Lê Thị Đức Hạnh and Xuân Tùng (Hanoi: Writers' Association Publishing, 1996).

[8] My use of the word "dames" in this context is explained below; please see "Notes on Translation."

[9] E. John Reinecke, "Tay Boi: Notes on the Pidgin French Spoken in Vietnam," in *Pidginization and Creolization of Languages*, ed. Dell Hymes (proceedings of a conference held at the University of the West Indies, Mona, Jamaica, April 1968) (Cambridge: Cambridge University Press, 1971), pp. 47-56. Reinecke states that in the century since the inception of *Tây bồi*, only a few papers have been written about the subject. The "language" seems to have become extinct with the departure of the French after 1954.

Legion) were "married" and "divorced" in this language. They went about their daily activities and interacted with each other through this means of communication, operating in this linguistic milieu even though they might not completely understand one another. Like their intercultural marriages, the intermixing of the Vietnamese and French languages crossed boundaries and thereby produced a new, hybrid language. By recording the sounds of a "kind-of-French language" rendered in a writing system based on Vietnamese phonetics, Phụng has recorded a new language that was spoken in the community of Thị Cầu at the time. This unique oral field of sounds, made up French and Vietnamese intermixed, seems to have been the language pattern for speaking and interacting in the village of Thị Cầu. However, this "kind-of-French language" does not appear to have been shared broadly across Vietnamese and French populations in Indochina in the 1930s,[10] though some Vietnamese apparently understood it; the author himself seemed to have been bilingual in French and Vietnamese, and he clearly understood it.

Situated in Bắc Ninh province, Thị Cầu was characterized by a few features which did not seem to be out of the ordinary in the landscape of Tonkin in the 1930s: it encompassed a hill and a train station located on each side of a river enwrapping winding rows of houses, like a water snake flowing downstream. Thanks to the foreign legionnaire camp and the activities involved in the "industry" of marrying the Europeans, Thị Cầu was a small hamlet redolent with international flavor that must have seemed extraordinary in this quiet provincial setting. It was a unique entity, a sub-society within a society, with a new language and customs of its own. The food eaten by the dames was undeniably made up of foreign imports: cheese, butter, sausages, Bordeaux wines, and so forth. Phụng remarked: "... imported cheese and butter have crossed the oceans to conquer people from a different social status." Other customs and traditions that were part of Vietnamese society were greatly altered in the Thị Cầu situation. In *The Industry of Marrying Europeans*, references are made to traditional marriage customs and practices having to do with ancestor worship, and the narrator shows how these traditions were executed differently by the dames in Thị Cầu; it appears that even though these Vietnamese dames had never left their homeland, they seemed to be awkwardly out of touch with traditional customs, as if they lived beyond the perimeter of Vietnamese society. In much the same way that the hybrid *Tây bồi* language differed from conventional French and Vietnamese languages, activities in Thị Cầu adapted and altered Vietnamese and French/Western customs, and these Vietnamese women lived and sustained themselves economically within the domain of the new *Tây bồi* culture. Their adaptations were not the results of emigrating and assimilating to a foreign country, since Thị Cầu is only a short bus ride from Hanoi, the capital and guardian of Vietnamese culture. Since neither the women nor their foreign legionnaire husbands were native speakers of French, and therefore no one in the community could be considered bilingual or bicultural, one might ask to what extent did *Tây bồi*, this French-based pidgin language, interrupt the continual development or awareness of Vietnamese culture in this locale? Cultural development for a society or an individual is influenced by languages, and as this mishmash *Tây bồi* developed, a new equally mishmashed culture, a "pidgin culture" of sorts, also arose from it, shaped by and shaping the lives of the people in the community.

---

[10] David G. Marr, *Vietnamese Tradition on Trial, 1920-1945* (Berkeley, CA: University of California Press, 1981), p. 147.

In Spanish, the term *"pocho"* describes individuals of Mexican origin who clumsily imitate Anglo-American speaking patterns.[11] In the subculture investigated by Phụng, the use of *Tây bồi* identifies individuals who speak French poorly, or who mix French and Vietnamese in their speaking patterns; as a result, this "kind-of-French language" serves not only as a linguistic marker, but also indicates a class distinction. The speakers of *Tây bồi* are associated with a general class of people who are backward, uneducated, and therefore inferior to the sophisticated French or the French-educated Vietnamese elites. Since many *Tây bồi* speakers were Annamite women who were married to the Europeans, they were naturally identified with this class. Even to the present day, when encountering *Tây bồi* in speech or in writing, a reasonably educated Vietnamese listener or reader would think that this "kind of language" is "funny," and would probably perceive the speakers of this "kind of language" stereotypically as unrefined, uncivilized, and barbaric. In other words, a reader who encounters this pidgin language would assume the narrator was describing a counterculture of lower-class origins.

The feminine of *pocho* is *pocha*. According to Guillermo Hernández, this term describes a Chicana who "traded one system for another without being able to enter successfully into her adopted world or to erase her identification with the one she's abandoning."[12] The Vietnamese term used to describe a woman who marries the Europeans and speaks *Tây bồi* is *me*. It is not exactly clear what *me* means, and the origin of the word has never been studied. It has been said that it might have derived from *madame* or *mademoiselle*. It might have derived from the Vietnamese word *"mê,"* which means "to be obsessed with." To the Vietnamese, the women who had liaisons with the Europeans at that time were known as *me Tây*, meaning "those who were obsessed with Westerners." Similarly, during the recent war with the Americans, the *me Mỹ* (America/American) women were seen as those who were obsessed with America/Americans.

Phụng clearly understood what was considered "civilized" or "uncivilized" in Indochina at the time. By choosing to record the speaking patterns of the dames and their husbands in *Tây bồi*, Phụng was able to illustrate class divisions in the society. The author repeatedly made references to the French spoken by the people he observed, especially when they did not speak nearly perfect French. It is apparent that Phụng was very conscious of the sounds of the "language" spoken by the residents of Thị Cầu, and his decision to write his report in these languages was more than a humorous device.

Because of this decision by the author to record what many perceived as the uneducated speech patterns of his subjects, it has been thought that Phụng shared the social sentiments of 1930s Indochina, and critics have accused him of being unsympathetic to the poor and oppressed.[13] I would argue that, on the contrary, this is an example of the author using incongruity as a comic device for the purpose of criticizing a society unsympathetic to the poor and oppressed. Phụng satirized the social world of the *me* by portraying it as a sort of refuse dump into which these women are "thrown" like a piece of unwanted goods. At one point, the narrator

---

[11] Guillermo E. Hernández, *Chicano Satire: A Study in Literary Culture* (Austin, TX: University of Texas Press, 1991), p. 17.

[12] Ibid., p. 19.

[13] Hoàng Ngọc Thanh, *Vietnam's Social and Political Development as Seen Through the Modern Novel* (New York: Peter Lang, 1991), p. 153.

states, "There, a person like that is only good for being around until one can find a way to throw her into the arms of the Europeans." This comment suggests that the first-person narrator, or the author, considers Vietnamese traditional values to be preferable to Western values, especially when they concern marriage. Whether or not the readers find "throwing her into the arms of the Europeans" humorous depends on the readers. One thing is certain, however—other references throughout the novel to Westernization and foreign foods and luxury goods carry a strong tone of criticism and satiric attack. Vũ Trọng Phụng's critical response to the dames' newly acquired taste for foreign extravagance was probably influenced by his own poverty and the harsh socio-economic conditions in Indochina at the time. Phụng was very aware of Western influences in the society, and this awareness was manifested through his observation of *Tây bồi,* this "kind-of-French language." On the one hand, he showed an appreciation for the Westerner's concept of beauty, an interest in things durable and well made, which differed from most Vietnamese products. Yet being an Annamite reporter, a victim of constant suspicion, Phụng was also skeptical about how Vietnamese society functioned under colonial rule, and his deployment of humor to imply disapproval suggested how ambivalent he felt towards his own contemporary society, which was neither Western nor Vietnamese, something he did not understand or approve.

Could satire be the vehicle used by an author reacting against or denying the emergence of the new culture? The writer constantly implies that crosscultural "activities" were neither appropriate nor acceptable, even though this opinion is presented as if in jest. Did Vũ Trọng Phụng intend to use satire as a tactic to mock people who had succumbed to European power? When answering this question, it is advisable to remember that the author was no less powerless than the people he apparently ridiculed. He was most interested in the people of the lower classes because his society was the least concerned about these individuals: the *me* themselves acknowledged that they were "society's discards," and the foreign legionnaires were portrayed as ex-convicts, without loyalty for France. Given that portrayal, it would be simplistic to view the legionnaires as vulnerable victims, the defenseless subjects of Phụng's cruel satire. Phụng used these individuals (including himself) for satire because they are the easiest group to make fun of, as the author himself indicated when asked why he would not seek interviews with dames who married French civilians or had secured a high position in society: "[If I do that] I will no longer have the freedom to continue to cajole and humiliate people." By "borrowing" these characters, Vũ Trọng Phụng was able to launch remarks aimed to criticize others. At one point the narrator comments, " ... to the *dames*, the bed was like a tool, like the baton to a policeman, a hammer to a carpenter, a neck to a congressman," implying that the Vietnamese congressmen would use their necks to nod greedily to the French. When the writer mocks men and women in the "industry," in fact his real purpose is to criticize other groups in the society, especially the Vietnamese collaborators and the rich members of the upper class, and those who worked for the colonial government and who quickly embraced the imported novelties of the West. Phụng reached for and found comfort in humor because it provided him a refuge from life under French domination.

More than fifty years since his death, Vũ Trọng Phụng's works still manage to perplex and fascinate everyone, from Vietnamese literary critics to politicians and revolutionary leaders. To read Vũ Trọng Phụng well, one must read what lies beneath the humorous exchanges that make up the text. What seems to be real to us is not real to the author. There is no doubt that he wants his readers to laugh, as he indeed deploys all the standard comic devices, with a clear mission of mocking his characters, including the "I" he plays. The reportage contains both true and fictional elements, and records the languages, the sounds, and lives of a rejected culture. The author, his character "I," and the rest of the characters of *The Industry of Marrying Europeans* intertwine and overlap like superimposed negatives of a once lively and colorful Thị Cầu society, long forgotten, but which comes alive when read. And the images that appear are only what we choose to see.

NOTE ON TRANSLATION

The majority of the reportage was written in *quốc ngữ*, the romanized Vietnamese script; the activities and dialogues among the women in the Thị Cầu area and between the author and the women are rendered in this language. All of the *quốc ngữ* texts were translated directly into English. As for parts that were written in "proper" French, I left them in their original form, with the English translation in brackets. Regarding the hybrid, "pidgin French" (or a "kind-of-French language"), I believe that it was the author's intention to record the actual sounds spoken by his subjects in a language that was not their native tongue. Thus, it is necessary that this (pidgin) language be kept in the original form, in the *quốc ngữ* transliteration of the French, with the Vietnamese diacritical marks, followed by the English translation in brackets. Since this is a French-based pidgin, it is appropriate to translate it into French as a bridge to English. As presented in the footnotes, this pidgin language is transformed into not one, but two forms of French. One is so-called "broken French," offered here to be consistent with the author's method of showing that this is not the language spoken by native French speakers. There are two small phrases in the original text that were written in both *Tây bồi* and Vietnamese *quốc ngữ*, so in those cases the Vietnamese and English translations are presented in bold, while the *Tây bồi* phrases have been translated into French (both forms) and English.

I would like to clarify several terms that I have used consistently throughout the translated text. In Vietnamese, the term *"me"* is used by some people to refer to women who "marry" Westerners. Since there is no English equivalent for that term, and "woman" is not specific enough, in the translation I have decided to adopt the term "dame" and use it solely for these women in question, to be consistent with Vũ Trọng Phụng's use of *me* in the reportage. As for terms of address, the Vietnamese language is very complicated when dealing with them. Numerous terms are used to address people, and they vary depending on the subject's age, marital status, gender, or relationships, familial or non-familial. Phụng used the term *"bà,"* which generally means "Mrs.," when referring to "older" women, and the term *"cô,"* or "miss," for younger ladies. To translate *"bà"* into "Mrs." would imply that the woman in question is married, whereas in fact many of them were not. Thus, in the translation, I have adopted the term "Madame" for the "older" dames.

Above all, I took care in translating this reportage because of Vũ Trọng Phụng's satirical narrative voice and intent. All translators, in essence, are second-hand writers. At some point the translator will have to interpret the original text and rewrite it into another language. In that process, the translator inevitably influences the interpretation, and sometimes changes the mood of the original text. Perhaps the most essential element when working on a satire is to capture its tone, not to provide a literal translation of the text. It is important to understand the author's intention, the context or the languages in which he chose to write. Tone is the voice of the author, and when translating humor it is not only necessary to understand the literal meanings of the words in the manuscript, but also to take into account the cultural aspects of the language, and most importantly, the mood of the author. Once tone has been captured, the translation is "alive," and then the mood of the translated text can be read or interpreted as it was intended by the author.

THE INDUSTRY OF MARRYING EUROPEANS

Vũ Trọng Phụng

1. HEAD AND EAR

The woman at the beverage stand was starting to tremble ...

In the face of someone who was stronger and about to give me trouble, no matter how unreasonably, I immediately stood up and moved back a few steps to get prepared. It's rather cowardly to pull oneself away, but it's best not to let it be known that you are right. Instead, I remained calm, and even acted afraid or respectful of the enemy because just my readiness alone would set him off.

The threats kept hitting me like hail ceaselessly thrown at my face:

"That's right. One hundred out of one hundred guys say that they have the right to come here. But they don't fool us. This Thị Cầu area is infamous for young fellows who come here and pick up women or do something shoddy. Those native scum! They're all suspicious-looking characters, just like you!" (Vũ Trọng Phụng's footnote: If you think those sentences are bizarre, please remember that I was trying to translate his French verbatim to capture the feelings of the speaker.)

The fellow who had picked a fight with me now made his hands into fists. His face reminded me of some character in the movie "The Big House." Sporting a beard of several days, he had that tough and rough look of Jean Valjean, when he had just escaped from the prison. But that seemed to be all he could manage to throw at me.

The fellow could not do anything more than spit on the ground, as he glared at me with his ferocious eyes. In front of me, he was like a tiger that wanted to roar. But my calm manner was like steel bars locking him in his cage. I waited for him to get bored with his anger:

"I am not one of those guys that a jealous husband has to settle the score with. Don't you be mistaken."

In the end, he grunted: "I certainly hope so. I warn you, if I ever catch you doing anything that brings shame to me or my mate, I will be at 'your service.'"

"Please do. And thank you," I quipped curtly.

Just like that, then he was gone. He walked away, clumping and leaving gigantic footprints on the muddy road. What kind of European was he? A German or a Russian? An Italian or a Belgian? Or a Pole?

I didn't know, and perhaps I didn't care to know all the details. All I could be sure of was the fact that a legionnaire was jealous at the sight of a young, strange man on his turf, which meant he had been cheated by an Annamite woman, one of those who married Westerners. (Vũ Trọng Phụng's footnote: "Westerners" here means Occidentals, so "married Westerners" means married Europeans, not only Frenchmen.) If you really thought about it, he had a right to be suspicious and pick a fight with me. Whenever a Westerner in Indochina met a Vietnamese journalist, he would immediately suspect the local newspaperman of working for an underground operation. When they saw an Annamite in Western clothing wandering about near their houses, the conclusion would be that the Annamite had one purpose: to seduce Western women!

The second reason was "The industry of marrying Europeans!"

Look at it this way: is the majority of courtship between local women and Westerners proper? Or is it, should I dare say, that perhaps it more appropriately resembles a type of "industry"?

Before I present evidence that might enable us to answer that question, I would like to describe situations that prompted me to ask this bizarre question.

In front of the main cathedral, Hanoi.

It was morning. The bell woke up the entire capital.

From the steps of the cathedral, forty cars lined up forming a strange gigantic snake wrapping around the block of Lagisquet Street: a European wedding. The sun was bright and shiny, bringing out the brilliance of the colorful outfits. People were mingling about, greeting each other as they stepped inside the cathedral. At one corner of the steps, a French family, 100 percent French, and a Franco-Annamite family were chatting livelily. There were only two people in the French family: a young and beautiful wife and her rather older, gray-haired husband. He carried the elegant stature of a prominent diplomat. There were four people in the Franco-Annamite family. The French husband, his Vietnamese wife, and their two children: one boy and one girl (of mixed race, of course). The sophisticated French couple delicately shook the hand of the "Westernized" Annamite lady. She was laughing and conversing in fluent French, and her manner was natural, and even elegant.

A scene like that would almost make us proud, that a woman—from a country that is still considered "barbaric"—still manages to maintain her dignity, even though she has been married to a colonialist. This is not an example of a woman in the "industry."

Let us observe another scene.

At one French house on the outskirts of the city. In the garden.

The local peasants were often surprised when they saw an elderly Frenchman in Vietnamese wooden clogs busy digging the vegetable patch, while at one corner of the yard his wife positioned herself comfortably in a rattan chair. Occasionally, she would look up from her knitting and talk to her mixed-race children in a jumble of Vietnamese and French; at times it was the language of dogs and cats, and other times a mixture of grumpiness and vulgarity. This was also a picture of a happy family, even though it contained the boorish talk of an Annamite woman. Perhaps the husband, a retired French soldier, had been accustomed to hearing cannons at the Battle of Verdun, so was not bothered by the uncivilized sounds of his language being slaughtered by this barbaric woman.

If that was all there was, I wouldn't be starting a reportage titled the "industry of marring Europeans." There is more.

One morning, in court, one Annamite *dame* said something that made everyone forget they were in the courtroom. The courtroom attendants broke into laughter as if they were somewhere else, watching a comedy show.

The translator had just finished calling her name. One broad approached the witness stand, swiveling her hips back and forth and clicking her heels as she walked. Her mannerism was rather out of place, impolite and rude, although she was quite a looker.

"What is your name?"

"Nguyễn Thị Ba," she replied.

"Age?

"Twenty-five."

"Your occupation?"

"First I was married to an assistant representative, later I got married to a ... "

"Be quiet! I asked about your occupation, not about your husband."

"Later I got married to a captain," she continued nonchalantly.

The translator quickly finished it for her:

"You don't have a job, right?" the translator asked the woman. "Unemployed," he continued as he turned to the judge: "*Sans profession.*"

"What do you mean unemployed?" the woman questioned the translator.

"What is your occupation then?" the translator asked again.

"What's my job? My occupation is ... marrying the Europeans!"

That prompted a roar in the courtroom. The judge stood up and motioned everyone to be quiet for a long moment, but laughter still echoed from the back of the room. The translator turned to the public prosecutor with this reply:

"*Elle déclare exercer le métier d'épouser les Européens!*"

[She states that her profession is marrying the Europeans!]

The public prosecutor looked at the tribunal president; the tribunal president looked at the prosecutor. Then, both of them cracked a knowing smile.

Her statement was quite humorous, but no less imprudent. Why would she dare to declare such a thing publicly? Or was there an occupation of marrying Frenchmen? Why did the lawmen smile? Did they empathize with her or did they acknowledge that her statement was not far from the truth? I certainly would like to understand the knowing smirks from those two lawmen.

The next day, in our famous Tonkin rain, a folder under my arm, cap in hand, I took the first bus to Thị Cầu district.

The *dames* divided European husbands into three categories: the civilians, the colonial soldiers, and the foreign legionnaires.

I wanted to go to the lowest lot first.

The road that entered the Cồ Mễ village would also lead me to the *dames*. I had just barely sat down at a roadside beverage stand, run by a "married to a European" *dame*, to dodge the rain before continuing on, when all of a sudden there came along that soldier picking trouble with me. It was certainly dangerous for a young, weak, and thin journalist to be in a place where these (European) husbands were jealous even of the Europeans.

Poor me, I only wanted to understand the smile of the two lawmen.

* * *

After the legionnaire's shadow disappeared behind the horse stable,[1] the café owner's face started to regain some color. Her relief was shared by another person: me.

"What did he want?" she asked.

"Oh, it's nothing. The fellow was jealous of me," I replied. "Why are you laughing?" I asked her. The beverage seller did not stop. And still laughing, she said:

"I knew it! Can't blame the fellow for being jealous. Just last Sunday, he caught her going out with another guy."

"Is that so!"

The woman continued, "That day, the fellow was a *săng-ty-nen* [*sentinelle*, guard], so he couldn't do anything. Later, the wife denied it and said that she went with her cousin to take care of family business. Fortunately, the fellow only gave her a few slaps."

Calling a few slaps fortunate? Dear Readers, please try to understand, the speaker was by no means unconcerned. If you think her statement was a joke, then you certainly don't understand her at all.

"Oh, by the way Mister, what brings you here?"

"I am a newspaperman. I just wander here and there and write whatever is interesting."

"Oh, good heavens! Now, can anyone blame that soldier?!" She is nodding her head while smiling deviously. Even the woman was suspicious of me. Immediately, I had to say something to redeem myself and show that I had no intention of shacking up with anyone here. I also asked her a few necessary questions. And thanks to our conversation, I had some general idea about Thị Cầu.

It was still raining hard. The woman was bored, and she decided to tell me everything. She told all.

There were only a few hills, a train station, and an army base, but Thị Cầu could be classified as an "international" province, just like the Thông, Tuyên Quang, and Việt Trì pagodas.[2] From its appearance, there was nothing about this place that could have an "international" atmosphere. But we should try to examine the souls of Thị Cầu.

Three hundred foreign legionnaires were stationed there, and there had to be many different kinds of Europeans. In one of those typical troops, a German would be standing next to a Russian, a Romanian next to a Portuguese, and everyone would be speaking broken French. Among those three hundred people, everyone was different, and each and everyone's accomplishment was just as remarkable. Three hundred biographies of darkness and anguish intertwined with each other. In order to have a better picture of their lives, one would have to see these films: *Le grand jeu, Je suis un évadé, Le passager*, etc. One of these guys probably poked a knife in some woman's beautiful ivory-white neck because she had committed adultery. Another probably shot his mother in the chest because she had cheated on his father. Another character probably stabbed a few guys because they were a touch anti-party. And then they enlisted and came here to forget or to look for whatever is left of life. In the old days, even if a foreign legionnaire was only a petty murderer, he could have been

---

[1] Vũ Trọng Phụng makes this reference throughout the novel, prompting the translator to assume that this was a place where people used to keep or raise horses. Otherwise, this house simply serves as a major "landmark" in the Thị Cầu area.

[2] Areas that were infamous for this kind of activity, the locations of the "industry."

a tiger once upon a time. He was fearless, and surely he had more guts than the average person. But once married to an Annamite woman, the holy tiger was as good as a caged animal.

If there were three hundred soldiers, that would make the number of *dames* to be around three hundred and fifty, give or take a few who were not working. Let's just say fifty "unemployed" *dames*. That would be sufficient for us to imagine the ugly scenes and petty brawls and trashy fights among the ladies. Then again, if the supply had not been more than the demand, the number of unfaithful husbands would not have been high. At first, I wanted to know only whether marrying Europeans was an industry, but after talking to the beverage-stand woman, I concluded that the industry was deteriorating.

Because the woman had told me:

"Last week, some women from Hanoi came here to look for husbands. They were married, but with a low salary they couldn't afford to buy the guys alcohol, cigarettes, and canned goods. Deprived and abused, they got scared and wanted a way out. See, marriage is proven to lose profit. What a waste! They've got talents, beauty, and even education, but see how they turned out. I can understand it if they were someone like me, but them? I've heard one of those city girls is working as a *ca-va-li-e* [*cavalière*, dancing girl] in some dance hall in Đáp Cầu."

Where was Miss Nguyễn Thị Kiểm? That could be some valuable "material" for her for a lecture [to her young protégés] on the problems of career advancement for women.

The seller continued her tale:

"There's something else that's ironic. These days there are a number of fellows who don't even want to get married. They just want to go drinking and gathering at those opium dens." I grabbed the opportunity:

"Do you know of any easygoing, unmarried fellows who might like to talk and perhaps might want to accept my invitation for a chat?"

"Sure! I know quite a few," she replied.

"I don't need many. One is enough. But he's got to be easygoing."

"Ah, then Corporal Dimitov."

"How do I make his acquaintance?"

"Wait until evening, after his duty, he'll definitely pass by here."

"You'll introduce him to me, won't you?"

"Sure! There's nothing to it! He's been married many times before, and all his wives all amount to nothing so he's really had it. He just wants to have an opportunity to express his grievance. If you want him to tell you all about the dirty business, then just degrade the females of your country so he knows whom he's dealing with. Just give the load! And you can invite him for a *cát-cút*[3] or to go drinking, or for a bowl of *phở*[4] ... whatever, it's up to you."

I told her when I would return and bid good-bye. She turned out to be a good-hearted woman after all, even though the sight of her smile with those white, bright teeth made my hair stand on end every time.[5]

---

[3] From the French word *casse-croûte*, which literally means breaking the crust of the bread. Vũ Trọng Phụng

[4] Vietnamese beef noodle soup.

[5] Traditionally, Vietnamese women had their teeth dyed black for cosmetic reasons. Those who had white teeth, who did not have them dyed, thus indicated that they were "modern" or Westernized at the time.

2. THE MATRIMONIAL WAR[6]

After two good sips of a local wine, my newly found, but "old," friend was quite drunk. Wine makes the blood warm, and warm blood makes us think about love, and love always hurts. Huddling around a weak opium lamp, in three hours, Dimitov confided to me the devastation of the Tcheka secret police.[7] In front of me, next to the opium lamp, lay a once courageous man, one who had dealt with the communists with hardened fervor, a "hero" of the Kerenski[8] government. Dimitov was a man of advanced age whose only dream was of a regime that valued the freedom of individuals, like the current French Republic. He left his country to go to Paris, and there he had been a chef in a grand hotel. Then came the kidnapping of Marshal Koutiepoff,[9] and Dimitov enlisted in the foreign legion. But these days, Dimitov was just a legionnaire soldier and an opium smoker.

"I've been to Tonkin twice, each time twenty-six months, meaning five years altogether. In five years, this is the first time I met a newspaper reporter. Oh, I'll tell you all. I'll tell you why a man like me has already been married fourteen times. And the Tonkinese women! My God! They truly are a bunch of skinny and dirty kids, in the words of French army poet De Vigny, 'twelve times dirty!' I am sorry, are you angry with me because I've said negative things about the women of your country? Probably not, because you need to know the truth. But if you are not happy, then please accept my apology."

"No, no! Why do you have to be sorry?"

Even though I had replied humbly, I felt satisfied beyond belief. Why did I feel like that? This hero wanted to humiliate a woman, and he was asking me for permission. I was just a humble newspaper reporter, but Dimitov probably thought I was some big shot like Pierre Seize or Louis Roubaud.[10] Then I remembered the events that took place earlier, when the woman at the beverage stand introduced us. I thought of her hand gestures and her incomprehensible French sentences, and how equally difficult it was for me to find ways to invite him out for a bowl of noodle soup. Now everything had changed. The wooden house on the street behind the horse barn was unwittingly hiding confessions of a general whose "heroic" achievements were no longer valued in Russia.

Outside, it was still raining. It had been like this for a week now, but at this moment the rain gave me a different kind of pleasure. The door creaked. The "shop" owner had just returned from an opium run. All we had to do was to move over and make room for others to get their fix.

* * *

---

[6] "*Cự môn thê thiếp*" in Vietnamese means "Multiple wives, stormy life." If one takes multiple wives, one's life is likely to be turbulent (with the wives or among the wives themselves).

[7] The Russian communist's secret police before the 1917 Revolution.

[8] Alexandre Fyodovich Kerensky (1881-1970) was the head of the Russian provisional government from July to October 1918 until the Bolsheviks seized power in the October Revolution.

[9] A general under the Czar.

[10] Famous French reporters at the time.

The Chinese horoscope had a phrase "Matrimonial war, happiness unfulfilled."[11] I am quite sure Dimitov was born with this destiny. The fellow had bragged about his fourteen wives, but only nine were Tonkinese.

"From now on, I am done with marriages. I have stabbed myself in the heart, the heart that bears so many heartaches, fourteen times to be exact. All of them cheated on me; each and every one of them did it differently, and in different situations."

"Please tell me the trickery of those nine Annamite women," I asked.

"The first woman was fat and not pretty. Before marrying me she had been with many men. Besides her European-style white teeth, she'd acquired a sense of worldliness, and that gave me happiness as well as pain. Happiness because I was waited on correctly, but I was in pain when I thought of those guys who shared her bed before me."

Here our dear Dimitov had to stop his pain to ... happily enjoy the first pipe, the pipe for the honored guest. After drawing on the pipe, he sat up:

"Really, I was never completely happy. I am a tough man, you know. I could strap sixty kilos on my body and walk thirty kilometers a day. But I didn't have the energy to exchange love words with her, so we fought every day. She yelled at me because I was jealous, I yelled at her for her promiscuity. One day, instead of serving Bordeaux wines, she had two bottles of cheap local wine, like the kind we drank earlier. Suspiciously, I asked and she said French Bordeaux wines were expensive and not good for me while the local wines were cheaper and better for my health ... So, I drank both bottles. And then, do you know what happened? You wouldn't know, would you? I certainly didn't. Only a few hours later, four patrolmen hauled me to a train station, and I was back in the barracks. The next day, after I had sobered up, I found out that I had destroyed a bicycle shop near the train station and injured a woman. Fifteen days in jail. No salary. At the end of the term I was released, but by then my wife had married someone else. The new husband, I later recalled, was one of the four patrolmen. Those bastards were probably in a conspiracy to get me drunk! I was so angry that I wanted to sue my wife, but when I went around and asked my comrades for support, all I received was mockery. At that time, I had just arrived, so I didn't understand the local customs. Some local customs, how interesting and how odd. Here, love between husband and wife is dictated by money. I was penalized because I didn't have the money to give my wife. This is no different than in the West: the court would just grant a divorce. That's not law; it's a custom. I didn't have the right to blame the woman who left me. You tell me, how can human beings treat each other like that? How can money have such power to weaken one's heart?"

Dimitov was thumping his chest as if he were really mad at me. But he didn't forget to lie down to receive the pipe from the den owner. Right, our Dimitov was very much in pain!

"There was nothing new about the second woman, and the third was the same," Dimitov continued. "I dumped them because they didn't understand French. Furthermore, they were ugly. My dear God! How stupid and ugly those two were! Do you know how the law of the stupid works? When you told them to clean the hat, if you didn't motion for the hat, they'd go polish the shoes. When you tell them to

---

[11] "*Cự môn thê thiếp, đa bất mãn hoài.*" This is a Vietnamese saying: One will always be unhappy with a stormy life of multiple wives.

buy unrolled cigarettes, they'd come with a pack of twenties! I sure didn't have the money for a translator. Yeah, they sure were ugly! We were only allowed to sleep at home three days a week, and those times when I lay next to my wife and looked at her face ..." Dimitov shrugged his shoulders, and stopped for a few moments.

"But it's safe to have an ugly wife. It's more dangerous when your wife is pretty. I don't know what the Europeans think, but we locals often say this," I opened the discussion.

"So you mean an ugly wife could bring you happiness?"

"Perhaps. I have never seen a finicky person happy."

"Yes, I am quite aware of that, but you're not being logical. If you have a beautiful wife whom you could trust, a woman who would never betray you. That would be an ultimate happiness. You're right, there have been times when I lay next to a homely woman, but I was proud. I was proud and happy because I trusted that she loved me and would never dream of sleeping with another man. Then, I would close my eyes. But when I opened to see that face ... oh, my, my ... Well, I tell you, you'd be so quick to embrace another philosophy: that it would be better to ... "

"It would be better to ...?" I prompted him.

"To have a beautiful wife who sleeps around." After having said that, Dimitov smiled at me. His sixth pipe was the ninth for the pipe server. It was still raining, and the wind was blowing harder than ever.

"What about the fourth wife?" I asked.

"Ah, the fourth one! The only woman that I left, but I regretted doing so. Even though she didn't speak one word of French, I still 'loved' her. We got along well. We didn't get along spiritually, how could we? We didn't speak the same tongue. We got along well ... physically. [And my God! What a lusty girl she was! With regard to the physical aspect, she had given me the illusion that she really loved me. Well, in life, what is better than our imagination? I almost forgot, she was a maid of my third wife. Don't you laugh at me, okay? A Vietnamese mandarin would never let his daughter marry a legionnaire. I am not embarrassed because she was a maid. In the West, it is nothing to be ashamed of if a nobleman sleeps with a maid. Anyhow, one day, she was 'unclean,' but she didn't say anything to me. A few days later, I was infected, and I was very angry. I wanted to scold her, but I gave her the benefit of the doubt that perhaps it wasn't her fault. Who knows? Perhaps the reason she couldn't tell me was because she didn't speak French. Then I decided to investigate a little. And it happened again. This time I asked her, and she could only nod. What a bitch! What a slut! I dumped her because I reckoned that she had lied to me. I thought because I had given her money I was the only person she slept with. It turned out that she enjoyed herself too much; she really took advantage of me! Really, she was the one who should have paid me.][12] Now that I have dumped her, I regret it. I will never find another woman with a fiery body like that. She could have been dead, and I wouldn't have even known it."

This fellow was either silly, or had an incredibly creative mind for criticism. The opium was finished; Dimitov was completely drunk and intoxicated. He lay helplessly. The opium server moved to a nearby hammock so that we could have more space.

---

[12] The material above enclosed in brackets appears only in the 1936 edition. I have not found it in any of the more recent editions.

* * *

"Please don't ask me about my fifth wife."

"How come?"

"Taking about her makes me sad."

"All right, let's talk about the later ones."

"Ah, I have to tell you about the four others. These four were good for nothing. And it was all their fault, too. You see—I am not the type who changes spouses like people change their underwear. This was my second time in Tonkin, so by then, I had learned not to get angry when something goes wrong. I understood clearly that they only did it for money. I had resolved that they would never understand men like us. So, this second time around, I treated them like long-term rentals. Never again would I misunderstand the meaning of the marriage vows. The sixth woman? Well, one night when I returned home from the base, I didn't see her, so I just left. As for the seventh, I caught her with an Annamite lover. The eighth dropped me because she couldn't get me to give her the amount of money she wanted. She couldn't manage the eighteen piastres I gave her per month. She dumped me to go off with someone else. That was not my fault. The ninth was a country girl. I raped her in Thái Nguyên. I remember, once she came here from all that way looking for me. How smart and clever she was. Pretty, I wanted to treat her like a wife. We were together for two months. One day, I saw some peasant fellow in my house, and she told me he was her brother. The next day, I was called to the court, and there, the judge pointed at my 'brother-in-law' and said I shouldn't be seducing 'another person's' wife. If I didn't let her go, they would court-martial me. [Who'd have known that she already had a husband?

"Why did you rape her?" I asked.

"Because when she was selling bananas, she behaved so ... well, like a whore."][13]

The bugle blew from the camp. Dimitov sat up, buttoned his shirt, tightened his belt, and put on his shoes. He shook my hand, and we decided that we would meet the next day. I could hear a woman's voice echoing into the room ...

"Dimitov! *Ven si* ..." [*Viens ici*—Come here!]

He quickly stepped out.

I looked at a fellow smoker. He answered me by shaking his head. One never understands the complicated love affairs of the legionnaires.

As for the person who had just left, my Dear Readers, please remember that once upon a time Dimitov was a "hero."

3. YOU DON'T CONSIDER ME AS YOUR HUSBAND ANYMORE?

Night fell. The sky was dark. The street was dirty. That basically described the scene on the road behind the horse stable at ten o'clock. I walked through the streets like a wanderer with an adventurous spirit. I was in total darkness. My shoes occasionally sank into the muddy potholes, and my ears were open to the rhythm of the horseshoes pounding on the pavement harmonizing with the neighs of the beasts. A strange feeling came over me, and I had a desire to rest peacefully like the beasts at the end of the day. How beautiful life would be!

---

[13] The material enclosed in brackets appears only in the 1936 edition. I have not found it in any of the more recent editions.

A light, finally! A flicker of light striving to illume the path, even though it was quite useless. It was a new punishment for my poor shoes because I could see that the better-lit paths had more muddy potholes than did the dark road. The tire marks crisscrossed like a pool of snakes on the dirt road. It is a curse for those who have a rich imagination because the thought of going through the small path in the middle of the graveyard, which was the only road to my friend's house in Cổ Mễ village, had just entered my mind. How unfortunate indeed!

I then remembered what the shop owner had said to me earlier: "It's getting late, why don't you stay over?" and I regretted [that I didn't accept the offer] terribly. But I just couldn't cry out, who would hear me? And the familiar barbwires on top of the red earthen walls that characterized Cổ Mễ appeared. Earlier during the day, I couldn't stop praising these walls because they seemed to possess the mystique of the type of houses in Tây Tạng;[14] now these haunting walls terrified me because I understood the meaning of that mystique.

Suddenly, a few yards from the wall, came a yell, and it sounded like an argument:

"*Toa ba mỏ nhá cút xê ăng co xê moa! Toa kích tê moa xăng bảy dề, a lò phi ní phăm, phi ní ma ghi. A-lô, kích!*"[15] [You have no right to sleep here anymore. You left me without paying. That's it. No more husband and wife. Go away! Go!]

A few silent moments passed. Then, the same voice of the woman screaming:

"*No, se phi ni! Văt tang.*"[16] [No, that's it! Go away!]

Twenty meters in front of me, in a wooden thatched house, under a faint oil lamp, stood the shadow of a soldier. The fellow was scratching his rib cage, his enormous body blocking the house entrance, yet one could see a rather imposing woman in white—white pants and white shirt, also as big as him, her hair messed up—giving him those lovely words.

The soldier—a husband or a client—was just standing there, testing her with his silence. The woman seemed to have lost her patience. She pointed to the door,

"*Va tăng! Ê tút-suýt!*"[17] [Go away! And right now!]

The husband who had just been rejected finally opened his mouth. Calmly he asked:

"*Re pét tơ cơ tuy viêng đơ đia.*"[18] [Repeat what you just said!]

The woman immediately turned to the man and continued:

"*Moa ba bơ toa! Si toa phe két sốt, moa điếc com măng đăng phe toa xếp linh ê toa pát sê công sây đơ ghe.*"[19] [I am not afraid of you. If you do anything, I'll have you court-martialed.]

---

[14] Tây Tạng means Tibet, but it is not certain whether Vũ Trọng Phụng, in describing these houses, is referring to Tibet or some place in Vietnam.

[15] *Toi pas moyen coucher encore chez moi! Toi quitter moi sans payer, alors fini femme, fini mari. Alors, quitte. [Tu ne peux plus coucher chez moi! Tu m'as quitté sans payer. Alors c'est fini, je ne suis plus ta femme et tu n'es plus mon mari. Allez, pars!]*

[16] *Non, c'est fini! Vas t'en!*

[17] *Vas t'en! Et toute de suite!*

[18] *Répète ce que tu viens de dire.*

[19] *Moi pas peur toi! Si toi fais quelque chose, moi dis commandant fait toi discipliner et toi passer conseil de guerre. [Je n'ai pas peur de toi. Si tu fais quelque chose, je le dirai au commandant et il te fera discipliner et passer au conseil de guerre.]*

Slap! The slap terminated those screams and yells. It also ended the threats. The woman moved back two steps and held her face in her hands. She lowered her head and stood there in silence. But, alas! The husband wanted the woman to talk more and talk louder and more forcefully than before. He had entered the ring; his fists were tightened. He had given her a "knuckle sandwich," but he wanted to continue until he got an *nốc ao* [knock out]. At that moment, the children were crying like screaming birds. Faster than lightning, a boy around ten years old ran out of the house. He went next door and pounded on the neighbor's door. Then out came two other legionnaires from the two adjacent houses. Still in pajamas and Vietnamese clogs, grumping and grunting, they poured into the center of the fighting zone. Three minutes later, the entire block of the horse stable was no longer quiet; women and kids were rushing to the battle zone to witness the spectacle.

I was busy looking at the spectators, and when I returned my attention to the main event, for some reason, things had taken a different turn. The "ousted husband" was thumping and kicking one of the neighbors. A minute later, another legionnaire stepped into the ring and started hitting the outrageous husband. Finally, one of them got a grip on the husband's hands while the other squeezed his neck. The unfortunate legionnaire slumped forward like a limp strand of hair above a fire.

Only then did I dare to get closer to the place. How strange it was! The women and children immediately looked at me quizzically, but those gents didn't even notice me at all. I don't understand how people could say that they are very suspicious.

At this moment, the wife sat up. She was breathing heavily while rubbing her face and massaging her back. She looked around, and, as if everyone surrounding her were her servants, she commanded:

"*Phe vơ nia ba tui!*"[20] [Go get the patrolmen!]

Suddenly, one legionnaire tapped my shoulder:

"Hey, you! Fellow! What are you doing here?" His voice was rude.

I put on a stern face, but still managed to control myself:

"I am not looking for trouble. I am a newspaperman, and I've come here to gather news." The legionnaire calmed down a bit:

"What kind of news? That was just a domestic quarrel between a husband and his wife."

"It looked like a murder trial was about to take place."

So this pleasant-looking and rather educated-looking soldier politely smiled at me:

"How would you comment on what happened earlier? What would you say about the legionnaire or the wife? Would you care to let me know in advance?"

Uh, oh. I am in trouble. A polite person is more dangerous than a rude person. An unrefined person might be hot tempered, but he is sincere, while a person who smiles at you politely will get you in the end. He is a careful schemer, and if he wants to teach you a lesson, then you've had it. I had to think carefully before answering him:

"In my country, domestic disputes are a common occurrence, so what is there to comment about? Perhaps I couldn't even write about that kind of news. I just think it's noble that you men withhold your fraternal friendship to protect a woman. How would you know if it might have been her fault?"

---

[20] *Fais venir patrouille! [Faites venir la patrouille!]*

The "polite" legionnaire is now happy. He shrugged,

"That's right. We Europeans cannot even use a flower to hit a woman. He hit a woman, and it's not good. He did something that is shameful to us. We are the stronger sex, so even if the woman is a nobody we'd still have to protect her."

At that time, four patrolmen arrived. The good neighbors who had been holding the husband to the floor finally let go of him. After the husband was taken away, everybody returned to their homes and went back to bed. I was surprised to see that everyone seemed to treat such a big event like a common occurrence.

And I could never forget the grunting smile of the ousted husband. Before the four *"ba tui"* [*patrouille*—patrolmen] pulled him away, he gave her a cynical and bitter smile that would surely promise the wife a blood bath. Before entering the house, I could still hear the woman's voice echoing in the background,

"Been *'công sây đơ ghe'* [*conseil de guerre*—court-martial] and still behavin' like that, this time I am calling it quits, ya hear!"

* * *

It was not clear what her name was, but the *dames* of the Thị Cầu society called her Madame Kiểm Lâm, so that was what I called her. She was eager to pull a chair for me, even though it was past eleven o'clock. Newspaper reporters had the reputation of snooping up dirt for money, but Madame Kiểm Lâm did not seem to mind talking to me after knowing who I was and what my intentions were.

Squatting on the bed, she dipped a cotton ball in a bowl of vinegar and rubbed it on her neck, cheek, forehead, and nose as she chatted. She was so comfortable and honest that I had to admire her courage for talking about something that wasn't too respectable. She didn't seem to be concerned about what everyone was thinking.

"Our kind is the no-good kind, dear Mister. Even if society doesn't denounce us, we know who we are. I am poor so I am not afraid of people laughing at me. I just want to get rich so I can get even with those who despise me. It's just that things are going backward for me. In the beginning, I fared quite well. I was married to a civilian like a decent girl, but when he returned to France I floated around for a while. Then, I got married to a soldier in the colonial regiment, and now, the foreign legionnaires, and things are still not going well. Long ago, when I was still young, I did get married to a decent man, you know."

My Dear Readers, the "career" path of the workers in the industry was indeed bumpy, muddy, and tortuous. Look at the achievements of us men; no one would receive a bachelor's degree, then a high school diploma, and an elementary school certificate in that order. However, one could compare this to the career path of a woman who is married to the Europeans because every husband, or to be more precise, every marriage has a value, like a certificate or a diploma, for advancing herself in the business. It is an occupation for her to sustain her livelihood.

Madame Kiểm Lâm hadn't dared to return to her village to visit her rich parents in a long time. She could have deservedly married a decent husband. A daughter of a rich family, she was also pretty; who would dare to think that she was going to be an old maid? And even today, her wind-washed face was still an image of a woman who once was beautiful. She could have had a peaceful life. What a pity that she was destined to have an amorous life, to have a heart that knew desire. Once upon a time, in her opulent youth, the young lady was in love with a particular fellow, but the two families were not compatible, hence the marriage couldn't go forward, leaving her so much pain ... and then, came one evening ...

A letter of farewell.

"I had thought about it carefully, and I didn't want to end my life. But at the same time, I wanted my parents to think that I was dead, so they would not be able to worry about me, even if they wanted to. From that day on, I've been leading a very adventurous, 'colorful' life."

Madame Kiểm Lâm flopped her head down for a while, and I thought she was crying. But when she lifted up her head, her face was tired and expressionless. How pitiful she was! Once a sensitive and compassionate young lady, but now her old heart could no longer be moved. She had become a beast in this society. Because a woman who has no tears left could be considered a beast.

"So, what was that all about?" I asked her, referring to the earlier commotion.

"Ah, it's all because of him. It's not my fault at all. Of course, we get involved with them for money, never for love. But sometimes, they are too much, you know. Sometimes, when they have money, they go find someone younger, and after they've spent all the money, then they want to return to us. How can you accept something like that?"

"I wouldn't think all of them are like that," I said.

"Well, some of them are quite kind. But that seems to be my fate; I seem to run into the good-for-nothing types. What can I do? That soldier was a German. In his country, he was a hit man and left it to come here. Don't you think we are brave, sleeping with murderers? He has a nice face, but his soul is evil."

Her voice was getting softer and her head was moving ... toward me.

One night, a legionnaire turned up the wick of the oil lamp. He looked at his wife's face carefully and asked:

"I am very good looking, aren't I?"

"Yes, very handsome."

"But, I have killed someone."

"Don't be a liar."

"Liar? Don't you want to know my crime?"

Then the legionnaire gritted his teeth and stared at his wife. Under the light, his handsome face had changed into a scary monster. Madame Kiểm Lâm was terrified; she screamed and turned her head to the wall.[21]

"Can you imagine someone who is so good looking that he could make you fall in love with him in one instant, but is terrifying to you the next? I have seen such a face ... two faces, as a matter of fact!"

She pointed at the three children who had been sitting on the bed and listening in:

"Ever since that time, I have always been afraid that one day in a rage of jealousy, he might kill those three kids from my three previous husbands. Tonight I had a reason to dump him, so why shouldn't I take this opportunity to get rid of him for good?"

---

[21] The dialogue, beginning with the sentence "One night, a legionnaire turned up the wick of the oil lamp," and ending with "she screamed and turned her head to the wall," seems to be the reporter's reconstruction or imagined version of what transpired between the legionnaire and Madame Kiểm Lâm.

It was midnight. The wind was blowing hard, but fortunately it was not raining. I stood up and asked her if I could come back another time. She saw me to the door and said:

"Please don't think that I am being too harsh with them. Even though I let him beat me, I am still the clever one. Had I admitted it, then one day he might kill me. I got married because of money, so they can forgive me for that. But if I admitted it, they would call me a whore. If your wife is a whore, then she might sleep with someone else who is more handsome when you're not home. You asked me about what happened earlier? Well, if I had said yes, who knows, he might have killed me instead of just hitting me."

I now know that there are people in life who are unusually thoughtful!

4. WIND [BLOWS], LEAF [RUSTLES], BIRD ON BRANCH [FLIES OFF][22]

The place "next door" could be called as such, even though the wooden house was not separated by a wall or by a partition. It was not entirely separated by a lattice either because only half of the fence was made out of lattice; the other half was a thin bamboo shutter. In order to have privacy, the landlady simply hung several paintings from Hàng Bồ Street with two rows of parallel couplets ... except in this case, hers didn't have the parallel couplets. So, from this side, if I paid close attention, I would have a good idea what was going in the "house" next door.

Madame Ách was still in the kitchen preparing coffee for me. I didn't know what Madame Kiểm Lâm had said to her friend, but I was moved by Madame Ách's hospitality. Luckily, at that moment she was out of a job, oops, out of husbands, and I could easily pass as her son, so no one was suspicious. Isn't that so? Even the most critical, the nosiest, and the most sharp-tongued *dame* wouldn't think that a young fellow like me would want to mess around with an old woman. I was most worried about Suzanne, her seventeen-year-old daughter. But fortunately, she had gone to Hanoi.

It's not that I am curious by nature, but when Madame Ách made my bed, she whispered: "Hey, there are a few *dames* looking for husbands next door." What was I supposed to do but take a deep breath and part the bamboo curtain to the side and poke my eyes in?

There were two *dames*. One was lying lazily reading an old newspaper. The other one sat emotionless on the chair, her arm crossed, shivering from the morning chill. Even her white pants, blue sweater, and peach flower socks couldn't hide a face that looks like ... a "*dame.*" Her teeth were white, but yet, how backward they still were! It was her calm and patient manner that I found most intriguing! Oh! Dear Sir, would you rise from the dead to see the face of a woman who has to sit around and wait for ... career advancement. How calm and collected she was. Then, please imagine the expression of someone who's waiting for a fish to bite the bait; I am sure you would admire the "philosophy" of this *dame.*

---

[22] "*Lá gió cành chim.*" Vietnamese saying that can be translated as follows: Just as the blowing wind causes the leaf to rustle and the bird perched on the branch to fly off and find a new perch, so the difficult circumstances of women without means of support causes them to move from place to place, from husband to husband.

A spoon clanged, and I turned around. Madame Ách had brought me a piece of bread and a cup of milk coffee. She called, and I went to the table. She winked at me and whispered:

"How many are over there?"

"Two."

"Only two? Then two others are not there. There are two dancing girls from Hanoi who just arrived a few days ago."

"They've come here to dance or to look for a husband?" I asked.

"Dance? Dance what? Probably looking for a husband," she answered. "Did you see anyone about my age sitting over there?"

I shook my head. She frowned for a moment and continued:

"There's Madame Cẩm. Back when she used to live in the Thông pagoda area, she was married to Mr. Cẩm. She didn't have any children, so in her later years, she became a 'madam' and lived off the 'interests.' Just like Madame Hai Yểng in this house. However, because she didn't have money she didn't fare as well as Madame Hai Yểng. Madame Hai Yểng had been in business for a long time; she had a successful *cát-cút* (*casse-croûte*) stand, and her bicycle shop was also doing well. Even so, a few ladies 'pulled the plug' on her and that was enough to send her into bankruptcy. How would a penniless Madame Cẩm survive? You're doomed if you don't have money and still like gambling!"

At that moment, there was a sound of wooden clogs thumping, and someone had entered the room. Then, one could hear people talking and chatting.

"How goes it, Madame, win or lose?" one *dame* asked.

"Won only three *sous*! I am so hungry! I saw a noodle stand, but I didn't dare to eat, afraid that I wouldn't have money for other things. Hey, look in the cabinet and see if there's anything. I think there's some bread left. Bring it out, and the butter tin too! Quickly! Hey, Duyên there, stand up and get moving!"

It seemed my dear Madame Cẩm had been disgraced by her habits. At that time, anyone with common sense would have asked for some cold rice and vegetable stew. But she was a creature of habit, after all. Butter and cheese have crossed the ocean and conquered all sorts of people on the social ladder.

Then one could hear Madame Cẩm screaming: "What's taking you so long? Don't you see the bread?"

A very calm, fearless voice replied: "Dear Miss, there is bread, but the butter tin is full of ants!"

"What? Ants in the butter? Damn you! You're only good for sitting around like my mother. You just don't know how to do anything right," shrieked Madame Cẩm.

Listening to one particular maiden named Duyên being scolded, I was very ... touched. I wanted to interfere. But I couldn't do anything at that moment. So I ran to the bamboo curtain and looked in. I guess that was some kind of consolation ... I did abandon my coffee!

The *dame* who had been lying on bed finally put an old newspaper aside and joined in:

"Hey, Duyên, look here, if you are so absent-minded you'll never end up with anyone decent. Look at me, even I still experience difficulties ... "

As if the forest fire needed more wind! Madame Cẩm continued to lash out at Duyên:

"Why didn't you stay in the village and marry some big country bully? How could someone like you dare to be choosy? I don't know what your parents ate to have someone like you! And your cooking—at least a couple of worms in every pan of your fried vegetables! And your hygiene—you don't wash yourself for an entire month—lice and ticks are all over the place! And your table manners—one cough and rice spits out like a rainstorm! Men should be choosy, but you? Choosy? As if you're gold or jade or something!"

Duyên stood there and lowered her head in silence. Not talking back was an admission of her mistakes. There! Somebody like that is only good for being around long enough until they find a way ... to throw her into the arms of the Europeans.

I returned to my coffee and thought about those legionnaires. Who were they? Were they heroes or criminals? Did they belong to a gang or a non-government party? Did they derail a train track to sabotage a diplomat's journey? Did they fire a few rounds at a local bank? Did they escape from jail while dodging the bullet sprays near the border? So that they could find their way to Thị Cầu and snuggle up with an object of so much desire and cry out: "I love you so very much, my beautiful!"

I didn't have the opportunity to see Duyên being selective about her men. Nor did I witness the times when three legionnaires dumped her. But with those peach-blossom-printed socks, that calm and emotionless, thick-looking face of hers, and those words of Madame Cẩm, I could almost imagine the life she had when she was still a country girl in the village:

[One early evening.[23]
Dear fellow strolling down the main road,
Kindly stop by so I can lament my troubles ... "[24]

Duyên was tying rice stalks in the field when she saw a man in silk pants, printed-gossamer shirt, and crepe-soled shoes, sporting a straw hat, a bamboo suitcase in hand, strolling casually on the main road. The fellow "strolling down the road" took a few steps and stopped. He looked at her. Other women were laughing from the rice field down below. Then, the man also started reciting:

Dear lady, destiny has determined so
Please don't flirt, for I have got a child,
But if you insist, my lap could be spared ...
My dear maiden, haven't you got a man?
Then, come climb up ... I let you carry ...
I let you hold.[25]

The women in the rice field were laughing louder than before; only Duyên stood there and looked down in silence. Duyên was married, and her silence was like a confession that she didn't love her husband, otherwise she would have found it funny.

The fellow "strolling down the road" smiled with satisfaction and walked on.

That night, at home, when Duyên lay next to husband, she felt so disgusted. Christ! He never washed his feet when he went to bed! What a stingy, dirty person he was. His table manners were also pathetic: he would always crouch at the dining table, so that his knees would always touch his ears. When he spoke, he stuttered

---

[23] This phrase apparently begins a scene imagined by the narrator. See n. 32.

[24] From a popular Vietnamese folk poem.

[25] To carry or hold a child.

incoherently. He was a nothing: the elderly hated him, the youths loathed him. What a bore! What a life!

During the next month, Duyên criticized her husband. The third month, she went to live with her sister. She and her husband mutually left each other.

So who would want to marry a promiscuous woman? Off Duyên went to Hanoi.

One day, at the capital, she ran into someone who resembled the fellow "strolling down the road." The fellow gave her plenty of nice, sweet talks. He invited her into the house to "chat" one night, and she agreed. The next morning, the fellow was nowhere to be found, and poor Duyên, she had taken off her silver earrings.

Then came the harsh life in the capital. Duyên couldn't take it anymore, so she crawled to the Thông Pagoda area to look for her aunt, a.k.a. Madame Cẩm.

"I beg you, dear aunty, I have been stupid." Even though Duyên admitted that she was being stupid, she didn't feel any remorse, not even a bit.

Madame Cẩm uttered: "What a tramp you are! What a wretch your mother was! All right, just stay here and look after me, and when it's convenient I'll give your hand to some Westerner."

The next day, Madame Cẩm threw the maid out of the house because she often fell asleep on the job. Then she taught her niece how to put on powder, part her lips, and pluck her eyebrows. Ah, Madame Cẩm loved her niece very much: she even took off a worn but still wearable silk bra and gave it to her. But she didn't forget to tell her not to wear it when she did the cooking and cleaning. Not long after that, all the *dames* in the Thông Pagoda district heard the news that a country girl named Duyên was looking for a husband.

One day, a *Monsieur Giăng* (Jean) stopped by: "*Ki e xen là?*"[26] [Who is she?]

"*Ma ni-ét. Bay dan, dơn, bô cu* **tốt**! *Toa vù lòa ê-pu-dê?*"[27] [My niece, peasant, young, very good. Want to marry her?]

"*Bay-dan? Vre? Đăng noa? Phét voa!*"[28] [A country girl? Really? With black teeth? Let's see!]

Madame Cẩm turned to her niece and gave a command: "Now look at him and flash a flirty smile! Go on!"

Duyên glanced at him and smiled. *Monsieur Giăng* nodded,

"*Xa và, xa và. Giơ viêng đê. Ô voa com me.*"[29] [Looks good, looks good. I'll be back. Bye-now.]

"*Chiêng! Giăng! Phô mơ đô nê vanh biết cẩm bua boa! Xăng qua ba lạp ben rơ vơ nia! Hánh?*"[30] [Eh, Jean, you have to tip me twenty piastres. Otherwise, don't bother coming back here, okay?]

Monsieur Jean nodded for a good long while and left. That was all there was to it. There was none of the usual marriage custom hoopla: two houses going back and forth, the engagement ceremony, the betel nuts, the rice cakes, the rice wines, the

---

[26] *Qui est celle là?*

[27] *Ma nièce, paysanne jeune, beaucoup* **good**. *Toi vouloir épouser?* [*Ma nièce, une jeune paysanne très gentille. Tu veux l'épouser?*]

[28] *Paysanne? Vrai? Dents noires? Fais voir!* [*Une paysanne, c'est vrai? Avec les dents noires? Fais-moi voir!*]

[29] *Ça va, ça va. Je reviendrai. Au revoir quand même.*

[30] *Tiens, Jean! Faut me donner vingt piastres comme pourboire. Sans quoi pas la peine de revenir, hein?* [*Donne-moi vingt piastres de pourboire. Sinon, pas la peine de revenir, hein!*]

wedding vows, etc., etc. Just a few imitation dog-meat[31] French phrases and that was all. Three days later, Duyên became Madame Jean. As for Madame Cẩm, she gained twenty piastres to put in her money chest. No profit lost!

{Monsieur Jean loved his wife even though she didn't understand French, even though she made a few mistakes. What did he really need anyway? So what if she wasn't very smart, not a brain in her head in fact. But, her voluptuous body was useful in some ways! Two months had gone by. Happy. Peaceful.

One day, Monsieur Jean wanted to brag to his buddies that he had married a peasant girl. In the middle of the party, she coughed and sneezed everywhere. He told her to spread butter on the bread; she didn't use a knife. Instead, she took an entire piece of bread and dipped it in a butter dish. After having had a bit to drink, he put a piece of cheese to his wife's nose; she couldn't stand the vulgar smell so she put her fingers to her nose and once again, she sprayed a round of food all over the house. His buddies looked at each other and shook their heads.

Next day, after he had sobered up, Monsieur Jean crawled to Madame Cẩm's house, complaining that his wife was ill mannered and a clumsy clod. There were a few "*bô cú tốt*" [*beaucoup* (very) good] things, but there were a lot more that were not so "*bô cú tốt*, etc., etc."

Duyên returned to live with Madame Cẩm.

Then came Monsieur Vendalie.

That day, he told her to make an "*épinard*" [spinach] dish. Well, she prepared it all right. It was very good, very good indeed. When he got through half of it, Vendalie saw one worm sitting happily in the middle of the plate.

Then came Corporal Dupond.

One night, he sneaked out from the camp to sleep with his wife at home. At midnight he had to get up to return to his guard duty. Three minutes before the duty time, and he was still not dressed. He asked his wife for a cup of tea. By the time she found the kettle in the darkness, tea leaves were stuck in the spout. In a hurry, she blew right into the spout and poured him a cup. He didn't drink the tea.

The next day he went to Madame Cẩm with this complaint:

"Look, Madame, I can't take the girl. It's a pity because she doesn't sleep around, but she's as dirty as a pig. I would rather have a wife who sleeps around than have a pig!"}[32]

Madame Ách told me quietly: "So what if Madame Cẩm yells at her? The girl doesn't need to get married. Every time she takes on a man, the aunty would take two piastres and the niece would keep one." If she does that ten times a month, the aunt would get the same amount as one marriage. And this is even better than having someone who demands all kinds of things."}[33]

---

[31] The Tonkinese were known for eating dogs. Sometimes, when there was none available, people would try using another type of meat and spices (usually pork and galangal) to imitate the flavor of dog meat (*giả cầy*). For the dog-meat connoisseur, *giả cầy* was a bad substitute for the real thing.

[32] The passage starting with the sentence that begins "One early evening" and ending with the sentence "I would rather have a wife who sleeps around than have a pig!" seems to be Vũ Trọng Phụng's imaginative reconstruction of Duyên's journey from being a country girl to being one of the "*dames*" in the big city.

[33] The material enclosed in curly brackets starting with "Monsieur Jean loved his wife even though she didn't understand French" and ending with "And this is even better than having someone who demands all kinds of things" appears only in the 1936 edition.

I was planning to go see Madame Yểng and Madame Sergeant Tứ, the queen who, together with Madame Ách, once ruled over the *dames*. I wanted to see if she still reigned over the industry as she once did in Việt Trì. I stood up and was about to leave.

"Hello, Mister."

"Hello, Miss," I answered her.

Suzanne had returned. She was dressed in the local garb. God! What a beauty she was! How could I go?

5. TO WANT OR NOT TO WANT: SUZANNE'S DILEMMA

Not only did Madame Ách give permission, but she also encouraged Suzanne and me to go out and sightsee in Thị Cầu and Đáp Cầu together. I didn't know whether she wanted to set us up or she trusted me. I will never know for sure, and I don't think I need to. Dear Readers, just take my word for it that a few hours after talking to Suzanne, I have become an understanding, compassionate, and generous being. I no longer look down on people.

During our outing, I asked Suzanne earnestly:

"You're going out with me, don't you worry about what people will say?"

Suzanne lowered her head and answered softly, "I think of you like an older brother, so whatever they want to say is up to them. I only know that I trust myself and that is enough."

When she said that, I was both happy and sad. I was happy because I was trusted, but sad because ... I was being trusted.

We went past the Võ Giang village, so on the way back to Bắc Ninh we backtracked. The weather was slightly cold, and it had just stopped raining, so it felt more like spring even though it was winter.

The *dames* ...

The *dames* ...

Encore the *dames* ...

We were not a newlywed couple, but there were so many *dames* rushing out to the doorways to watch us walk by, it was as if there was a wedding in progress. Looking at their white pants, white teeth, sweaters, and vests makes me want to ask them: "A lot of time on your hands, eh? Why don't you get together to play a few games of cards?" Whether they were good-looking or not, their faces were very difficult to describe. They were standing by the doorway, half-hidden behind the bamboo lattice, and all of a sudden, I wanted to change the lyrics of Ôn Như Hầu's poem:

Shadows flicker behind the curtains,
Even trees and grass were afraid of a storm.

"Many *dames* are old and ugly, but how come they are still so popular?" I asked Suzanne.

"Ah, I know the answer to that very well. The Westerners' concept of beauty is different than ours. When you see a big, fat and well-endowed woman, she might look scary to you, right? But the Westerners think she's pretty. Do you know Madame Bé Tý? I've heard a European say that she was a complete beauty, the most beautiful woman in Annam. But when you see a waif, you would helplessly fall in love with her, right? The Europeans think that kind of beauty is sickly because after a few childbirths that would be the end of her. Secondly, that kind of frail beauty doesn't last. Don't you agree?"

I smiled and asked: "So, do the Europeans want to buy durable goods, something that they can keep for a long time?"

Suzanne slightly gave me an elbow right into my love handle: "Mister, when you buy something, say furniture, or when you have your clothes made, would you like your goods to get worn out or fall apart quickly?"

That explains why the Europeans like sports and why the things that they create are not only beautiful but also durable. In the East, the Japanese for example, they only cherish things that are fragile and beautiful but fall apart quickly.

Suzanne's explanation gave me a new perspective on the two views of beauty. But I still wanted to know how did those ugly-as-a-ghost *dames* manage to get married? And speaking of ugliness, Madame Ách was definitely in that category. So, then, how am I going to ask her? I went in circles:

"Perhaps to the Westerners, beauty isn't the only thing that matters. Some of them probably have a high regard for personality, and they probably want to have a decent, virtuous wife. That must be the reason then, so those ladies who are not exactly beauty queens wouldn't do so badly after all ... "

Suzanne turned out to be better than I was: She was honest. She continued:

"That's what you think. Proper morality is something that women who are married to the Europeans would never be entitled to. Why would the Europeans marry even the ugly and the old? Because these Europeans have nothing left in life to look forward to. If they kept a servant, they would be worried about having things stolen. It's better if they are married to the local women. They can give orders however they please, and at the same time ... their needs will be taken care of. They don't speak the same language, and if the wife's reason for being with him is his bank account, then how easy do you think it is for him to express his affection to her? Furthermore, no one knows what they did, what kind of life they had before they came here. Surely they didn't come here to look for the love of their life. When two people have the same level of social status, are intellectually compatible, and need and love each other, that is love. If you want to have love, then neither side should be in the position where one would look down on the other. In the case where two people's incompatibilities are so great that the so-called love is not true love, what they have is human compassion."

Even though Suzanne was very young, how well she understood life! Unfortunately, that is not necessarily a good thing. Those who understand life well are not often happy. Happiness seems to happen to those who don't know what life is all about.

We had gone a good distance on the dirt road. We passed the hospital, the hill, the train station, and now in front of us lay a bridge and a river. To the left was a railroad track, and the artillery barracks were on the right.

"Should we go up the hill?" I asked.

Suzanne nodded. As we walked around a brick factory and rows of houses behind the Đáp Cầu market, we casually marched up the hill. The houses in this area were so different that I felt as if I had traveled to some strange place. The roofs of red earth houses, some high, some low, crowded in and stepped on each other, and were separated by winding paths that wrapped around each other like snakes, as rocks and green moss intermingled like a step ladder climbing up a mountain. It was certainly breathtaking!

Now, this was the right time to find out what was on the mind of the young and pretty French-Annamite girl. I wanted to know if she had made any plans for her future. And of course, those heart-to-heart moments could only be entertained by an enchanted view. Small temples were scattered about while guava trees ornamented the landscape of the hill. At the foot of the hill, a group of houses was situated near an army camp while a river flowed quietly to the side. Quite poetic, no?

"Even though I have French blood, I don't hope to marry a Frenchman. That would be the last thing I would do. My mother has been remarried four times since my father returned to France. I have seen and understood everything. If I were married to a Frenchman, I might have to follow him to the ... motherland, and I can't bear leaving my mother here to die of hunger."

"So marry an Annamite," I commented.

"That's not so easy. If a guy dares to ask for my hand, probably he won't get his family's blessing. I am not sure if we can bear that kind of criticism. Furthermore, if they just like me for my good looks, then when they are tired of me, they might leave me. And I am talking about those who have guts. As for the fellows who lead a respectable life, they wouldn't be brave enough to marry a mixed-blood girl. What a doom to have been born a Eurasian. The Europeans don't respect us entirely, the Annamites won't love us fully. In the respectable Western society, a drop of Annam blood is a disgrace, and to the noble Annamite society, a drop of French blood is not quite an honor either. Oh, my God! That means I don't have a country!"

Suzanne put her head down and began to cry.

I pulled her closer, and I wanted to show my emotion with a kiss. But I didn't. I had better not play with fire.

Suzanne bitterly repeated that sentence: *"Oui, je suis sans patrie"* [Indeed, I am without a fatherland.]

I said quietly, "You can marry a French-Vietnamese."

Hiding her agony, she said calmly:

"You're right. I have thought about it. A Eurasian would also have French nationality, and he couldn't hate me. If he is rich, then I'll dress like a Westerner, if he is not, for example, if he's a soldier, then I'll dress like an Annamite woman. I used to study at a school for unwanted Eurasians. If I didn't think about my mother, I would have gone to France a long time ago. If I had wanted to marry a civilian like any decent girl, then I would have stayed in Hanoi. I would have worked as a cashier and earned about twenty, thirty piastres a month, and perhaps I would have even been married. But I would rather live with my mother, to share her hardship, her poverty, and together we will eat corn and potato."

And that was how Suzanne got over her pain. Her filial piety to her mother had made her into a heroine. She continued, "Why should I feel sorry for myself because I don't have a country?"

After having said that, she stood up and looked around the hill.

Suzanne didn't want to marry a Frenchman, and she was not hurt because she didn't have a fatherland to worship. Still, she didn't want to marry an Annamite. What fun was there left? I wondered if that could be possible.

I acted indifferently: "I think marrying an Annamite is still better ..."

She glanced at me with a smile—an endearing smile at that:

"Ah, my mother has always said so. She said she wanted to have a Vietnamese son-in-law to take care of her burial when she's gone. She is worried more about dying than living."

How fortunate! I seized this good opportunity:

"That's right! Your mother is right. Suzanne, you should get married to a Vietnamese; just look for someone plain, but noble, someone who has an open mind, who has a new perspective on our society and will not be concerned with the traditional and outdated ideologies. Someone who only cares about love."

She smiles: "Like you? Well, that's all Bưởi school talk.[34]

I also smiled, but Suzanne quickly changed to a serious tone:

"You know, that's impossible. We always dream that life is good and beautiful, and despair would not exist as long as we had good fortune. Actually, it lingers and happens in the end. Take the son in-law of Madame Đồng Đền in Phủ Lạng as an example."

This story should belong to this reportage of "the industry of marrying Europeans," except in this case, the worker is a male. There was this character who treated his wife like a gold mine. Suzanne told me the story in three minutes, but it took me more than thirty sentences to get everything down.

About eight years ago, there was a schoolteacher who was accused of having a romantic interlude with a French-Vietnamese woman, the only daughter of Madame Đồng Đền. The entire province called him a "gold-digger" because Madame Đồng Đền was quite well off. Furthermore, she had spent loads to repair a temple in the North Gate market.

["How did she get to be rich?"

"Was she in the opium trade?"

"Nah, she inherited from her husbands."

"Liar, she's ugly as a ghost, and you're telling me she got rich from the business of marrying Europeans?"

"Pretty or not, it doesn't matter, it's all fate."][35]

That basically was the gossip from the *dames* who were jealous of Madame Đồng Đền's good fortune. But you can't blame them, for Madame Đồng Đền's extraordinary biography was enough to tantalize the *dames*.

When she was younger, she was known as Tư Bạc because she wanted to partner with a soldier, someone whose sense of aesthetics hadn't fully developed.[36] From that liaison, a baby girl was born. And then one day, while Madame Tư Bạc was pondering about life, she lamented: "O river, dull river, there thee went ... when shall thee return?"

A few years passed. The deprivation, the humiliation, she had no choice but to take on the "bird-perched-on-a-branch" lifestyle.[37] One night, a major and a

---

[34] Bưởi School was an elite school for boys in Hanoi.

[35] The dialogue beginning with the sentence "How did she get to be rich?" and ending with "Pretty or not, it doesn't matter, it's all fate" seems to be another of Vũ Trọng Phụng's imaginative reconstructions, this time about the *dames*' gossip about Madame Đồng Đền.

[36] "*Bạc*" in Vietnamese means silver and "*đồng*" means copper. One possible explanation of this passage could be that when Madame Tư Bạc was younger she was "gleaming" and "shiny" like silver, but later in life she became duller, hence the nickname. "*Đền*" means an altar or temple. Madame Đồng Đền's name could be interpreted as indicating that Madame Đồng Đền devoted her later years to fixing and going to her favorite temple.

[37] See n. 22.

physician called for her. Next month she became Madame Major. Was it love or was it compassion? Who can really understand the generosity of a man? Just say it was destiny. A few years later, the major went back to his country and never returned. Next year, another major knocked on her door. He, too, also went home not very long after that. They all left her rows of brick houses and enough money to fill a trunk. Then, she decided to abstain. But, since she had only one daughter, she wanted to have a Vietnamese son-in-law who could take care of her burial later on. One day, a schoolteacher came to her house and proposed to her daughter: "I will marry you because of love, never for money." Everything was rosy for a few years. Now, the beloved son-in-law would spend all day praying for his mother-in-law to drop dead.

Julie, his wife, scolded him: "What a scum! You only think of money."

The husband laughed: "To be your husband is a humiliation, to be your mother's son-in-law is a humiliation. And if I can't even think about the money, then people will be sneering at me."

Granted, Madame Đồng Đền was quite aware of the attitude of her beloved son-in-law. But did she care? There she was, night and day at a shrine praying to the goddess of mercy.[38]

"No! Rich or poor, I am not going to marry an Annamite," Suzanne sighed.

I also sighed.

* * *

"Yes, I have to go right away. Madame Kiểm Lâm has called for me."

"Before returning to Hanoi, are you going to come back here?"

"I really don't know, so I won't dare say. I sincerely bid you and Miss good-bye." I took my hat and left.

"Oh, Mister," Suzanne ran after me.

"What's the meaning of this necklace?" She asked me earnestly.

On our way home, I had stopped by a Chinese store on Chính Street and got her a crystal necklace. I waited until we got home and timidly put that on her neck. Madame Ách was poor, but she had gone out of her way to treat me. Then when asked, I had to blurt out:

"A very painful souvenir."

I hope someday these words will be under Suzanne's eyes.

6. THE LOVE LETTERS

Madame Kiểm Lâm had introduced me to Madame Corporal Bu-Dấch [Bougique], but she didn't invite me to her home. Instead, she asked me to go to the house of one of her "colleagues." According to the directions on a ripped-up dry cleaning receipt, I should go to a house that has a wire gate on the street of the horse stable.

---

[38] The practice where many socialites would go to the shrine to sing and dance. A form of entertainment or social gathering among these women (*lên đồng*).

I had merely stepped my foot into the yard, when a voice of a woman could be heard from the house:

"*Bạc đồng me sừ* **chớ có mà** *phát xê.*" [Excuse me, Mister, **please don't** get angry so quickly.][39]

"*At tăng moa rắc công tê tú xa.*"[40] [Please wait until I tell you everything.]

Every place has its own poetry. Here, because it was an amalgamation of East and West, the poetry seemed to be more civilized than ours; certainly more civilized than the poetry in places that would have no electric cars.

I wanted to listen more, but the footsteps were already at the front gate.

"Please come in, we sisters have been waiting for you."

That was Madame Corporal. I tipped my hat, then followed her, entering the room. The entire place was one multi-function room: living room, dining room, and bedroom. It could also serve as an altar because on top of the cupboard next to the Western bed was an object displayed on the worship area: a picture of a tiger. I wondered whether or not the king of the jungle knew how to eat butter. Who played a trick and put out a tin of butter as if they wanted to offer it to the lord?[41]

Two *dames* were on the bed engaging in a game of cards. If you think about it carefully, that bed was not only a gambling table, but it had also witnessed many amorous wedding nights. Who knows, probably it was also an accomplice of many adulterous affairs. To the *dames*, a bed was like the baton of a policemen, the hammer of a carpenter, the neck of a congressman. In the industry of marrying Europeans, the workers worked on a bed.

Seeing me walking in, two ladies started to gather several pairs of white shorts into a pile. They motioned me to sit ... on top of them. One lady asked Madame Corporal Bu-Dích:

"Is he the one?"

"Yes," Madame Corporal answered.

That lady smiled and continued: "So, are you planning to dig up our dirt for your paper?"

"No, I won't be dirtying anyone. I just want to know the truth," I answered.

Madame Bu-Dích interfered so as to show who was the boss:

"Don't monkey around! Do you think he came here to joke with us?"

I had to choose my words carefully:

"Please, understand. We only want to know about the relationships between the Annam women and the European men, whether they are turbulent or peaceful. We are also most interested in the offspring of these unions. There are quite a lot of them, and I am sure they will pose a problem for our lawmakers in the future. As you know, our society seems to think that the only reason you women marry the Europeans is for money. I wonder if there are any who married for love?"

From my statement, I would never have expected the *dames* to raise a storm. Both immediately attacked me:

"No? Why wouldn't it be for money? Just think about it: how would it be possible for us to marry them for love? Furthermore, to them it is certainly not for

---

[39] *Pardon monsieur* **chớ có mà** *fâcher. [Pardon monsieur, ne vous fâcher pas si vite.]*

[40] *Attends-moi raconter tout ça. [Attendez que je vous raconte tout ça.]*

[41] A typical Vietnamese altar would have pictures of the deceased, incense, tea, and some food items.

love! We are simply their long-term toy dolls." They seemed to be very satisfied after having said that.

Really, I could not imagine. If I had tried to flatter them by saying otherwise, they would have known straight away that I had ridiculed them. But, among thousands of ladies who had married the Europeans, could all of them be like that?

All of a sudden, one woman said:

"If you are going to write in your paper, then you might as well write the truth, that we marry them for money. Because our kind is no use to the society, and it need not to be concerned with us."

Wait! Well, then in the campaign of the conglomerate of East and West launched by the colonial governor Phó Nam Vương, the *dames* were one of the first to be sacrificed. Couldn't they be at least recognized for their achievements?

Again, I had to watch what I was going to say:

"If all of your love affairs could be documented in a history book, I assume there have got to be some ladies who have done something noble?"

Madame Corporal Bu Dích replied right away:

"The first Tonkinese woman who married a Frenchman is Madame Sergeant Chóp. She was the 'founding mother' of this occupation. The sergeant has passed away, and these days she is neither rich nor poor. She doesn't have any children, so she's taken up another occupation, something that we often consider 'charity work': she is a hired crier."

"Oh, my! hu! hu! How could you leave me? How could you leave your family, your parents, your relatives, your houses, and your neighbors? How could you? hu! hu!"

Forty years ago, the occupation of the hired crier was born. Their job is to "help out" at funerals so the departed one could feel loved. So if there was a family who felt that their mourning cries were not loud enough for the deceased, Madame Sergeant Chóp would be "invited" to give a helping ... mouth. Madame Sergeant Chóp, a generous soul, would be glad to cry. She cried happily, cried meticulously, and at no charge, meaning she even cried *ga-tuýt* (*gratuit*).

Never mind, let's just hear what Madame Corporal had to say:

"Our country has thousands of unwanted Eurasian children, and the number of young men and women with French nationality is also up there. All of that crime and those achievements started because of Madame Sergeant. She had the courage to pass it on to her successors that we should not be afraid of those red-haired, blue-eyed giants, who speak with their arms and legs as if they are about to pick a fight. You see, whenever we were afraid or hesitated to share our bodies with the foreigners, the ghost of our founding mother would appear and say: 'Don't be afraid, the Europeans are civilized, they don't eat us. Go ahead, sleep with them!'"

None of us could stop laughing. That was Madame Corporal for you. Mind you, her husband had just dumped her a few days ago, so she probably had just experienced some ugly battle. And she still could find humor even at a time like this. That tells you her heart is immune to pain. To her, getting married or getting divorced is just like owning dishes: if one breaks, so be it.

At this time, a group of her children came into the room. They all looked kind of "neat," quick, and clever, unlike other children. There was a three-year-old who looked exactly like the child in the printed ad of the Bird-brand milk.

Suddenly, I thought of their parents, and I felt sad. What is going to happen to them? What have they got for their future? Suzanne's words seemed to be floating in and out of my head, incriminating.

"Mom, look at what Jean did. He picked up a toy anchor and wore it on his bib," said a little girl while pointing at her younger brother.

"Go away! Don't you see I have company? Don't come in and disturb me." After scolding them, Madame Corporal raised her wooden clog up in the air. The children were terrified and quickly pushed each other out of the room.

Could that be possible? Regardless of how monstrous a woman has become, a mother would never be that vicious to her own flesh and blood. Why did Madame Corporal treat those cute, sweet kids like a warden treating his criminals? I wanted to interfere but, fortunately, I understood.

While the woman thinks about money, the man thinks only about physical pleasure. There seems to be a wall between them, and no honest communication can get across it—any true affection would be mistrusted! Unfortunately, not everyone was brave enough to use contraceptives. And the result of those ... interminglings is what we just saw. To most couples, having a child is a blessing, but for these couples it is a curse. For the woman, it seems that after she gives birth, she is filled with regret. And for the man, if he doesn't have regrets, then he drives himself insane with the inevitable suspicion: Is it mine?

The innocent kids are the ones who receive the bitter punishment, whether it springs from their parents' suspicion or regret. Those pitiful kids truly deserve love. But, what is it to Madame Corporal? She doesn't give a damn if they are other people's children or her own. She is just like the government! (Phụng's footnote: Since the depression, the government no longer places priority on helping the unwanted Eurasian children.)

She continued with her stories nonchalantly:

"Even though Madame Sergeant Chóp is known for being the first in this industry, you couldn't really say that she is honorable. Being a hired crier—how noble could that be? In our business, the successful ones are very few: Madame Tây-Cú, Madame Chanh-Ty, Madame La-Oa, and Madame Đuy-Kiêng. Also, there are a few who are married to civilian administrators and businessmen. There you have it. But would you dare say that any of them had actually married for love? Well, rest assured: when a woman is married to a European, everybody in her family benefits."

Two more *dames* walked in. The one with Western-style, high-heeled shoes and a trench coat was talking loudly:

"Gee! The Bôn girl is in high demand, but she's such a bitch!"

The second *dame* threw an umbrella on the table and said:

"Look out! I am going to give her a snap, and she will be her own self again. You all remember the story of the girl with François?"

It must have been an insider's joke because they all cracked up laughing. Madame Corporal turned to a *dame* who had been sitting quiet:

"Go ahead and ask him to write it for you." Then she turned to me, "Please excuse me, Mister."

Then, they all headed to the card table. One *dame* didn't join them; she pulled me to a table.

* * *

From a Japanese tin, she pulled out five pictures and a bundle of letters. I had thought the tin was for betel nuts. Among the five pictures, two were pictures of her eight-year-old daughter and the other three were photos of her three husbands. There was also a little notebook with a green border.

"Mister, among the sisters in the industry, only I can be proud that I have the least number of husbands. Considering the number of years, I've had only three husbands. Furthermore, I had some education. But in the case of important business, I think it'd be better to ask for your help. I am afraid they would laugh at me because of my broken French."

This *dame* wanted to "take another step," and she was planning to send her daughter to the organization for mixed-blood children. She continued,

"After she's turned sixteen, they will find her a job here or send her to France. She's a girl, so what's the use of keeping her? If she were a French citizen, it would have been worth it. Unfortunately, when I gave birth to her, I told both of the husbands. I didn't know which one was willing to be her father, and that's what I did. What would I do if they both found out and wanted to kill me?"

I pulled out my pen and was quite happy to start constructing the letter for her, but this tricky woman wanted to tell me more about the "tricks" that she used to lure the two legionnaires:

"This is my second husband ... and this picture here, is the third. The second had a bushy beard, but he was very nice. This handsome fellow here, on the other hand, was very clever and cunning. But he couldn't outdo me, I am not stupid, you know. Actually, being literate does have an advantage. I just hit on the emotional side, then they'd all fall for it. If only I had finished elementary school, I would easily have gotten a few more in my traps."

Then she gave me the notebook with the green cover.

"What is it for?" I asked.

"That has all the letters that I have written for those two."

"Why bother keeping copies like a merchant?" I asked.

"Why bother? If you're cheating them and don't bother to keep records, then sooner or later your story will have a different ending. What am I going to do when there's no money?"

"So, these two men are not here now?"

"The old guy is with the colonial army, and currently he is stationed in Marseilles. His doctor says this place is not good for his health. The young one was transferred to Africa more than one year ago. But they still send me money for my child."

I opened the letters of the old husband. One of them had the following:

"You are the dearest person to me. I am in pain for leaving you because of my illness. Jeannette looks very pretty in the picture. I like it very much. I am very sad to be apart from her. I have been drinking a lot these days because I am terribly depressed. Please try to write often. I have enclosed a check for one hundred francs. A hundred kisses for my daughter, and a thousand kisses for you."

And the letter from the young fellow who is stationed in Africa:

"This country is so hot and the women are so ugly! I don't feel bad shooting the commie rebels. Sometimes I worry about getting stabbed in the back and that would end the hope of returning to Tonkin to be with you and Jeannette. Alas! I don't know when death will come for me. I think you might as well remarry. But you should find someone who's willing to be a father for our Jeannette, so that she won't be illegitimate, etc., etc. ... "

But here's the letter "she" wrote to the old man:

Je suis mort de faim mais je ne pense pas d' épouser un autre mari. Les autres personnes dangereux. Moi e[s]t c'est pas qui! Pas possible quelqu'un honnete comme vous, mon vieux cher. Alors, Jeannette reste sans papa, mais je mens fouts, n'est ce pas? Envoyer moi de tant en tant d'argent et votre fille serons heureuse.

[I am dying of hunger, but I am not thinking about getting married to another man. Everyone else is dangerous. I am not just anyone. No one is as honest as you, my dear old man. Jeannette will not have a daddy, but I don't give a damn, right? Please send me money from time to time and your daughter will be happy.]

And here's the letter "she" wrote to the young man:

Jeannette ne voudrait suivre son papa. Elle pleure toujours. Je l'ai fait voir photo de vous. A Tonkin, c'est la crise d'argent. Ces habits sont mauvaise état. Je veux dire vraiment: si vous êtes impossible à m'envoyer beaucoup d'argent, je pense épouser encore un mari ...

Votre femme, Thị B. Très chérie.

[Jeannette will not follow her father. She cries all the time. I have let her see your picture. There's an economic crisis in Tonkin. Her clothes are in bad shape. I really mean it: if you can't send me a lot of money, I am thinking of taking up with another husband.

Your wife, Thị B. Very dear.]

I wanted to laugh. The obscene thing was that she almost jumped up and yelled:

"So, you see how scheming we are. Please don't ever be mistaken that we marry them for love."

Oh, really? How strange that you need to prove yourself. I picked up my pen and started writing. I was neither sad nor did I want to laugh. It was a pity that I didn't have my camera.

7. WHO WANTS TO BECOME A LION?

Thế Lữ's old tiger in the zoo wanted to roar, "O, where now are those glorious times?"[42] Even though she was once a tiger—or a lion—but now old and retired, Madame Sergeant Tứ would never lament like that. Indeed, her glorious times were now gone, but she has done something that was equally glorious: she has passed her knowledge of the trade to her naive protégés. Once her name was mentioned, all the *dames* at Thị Cầu seemed to treat her with a great deal of admiration: "Our sister Sergeant Tứ is one in a million, however tough or rough these guys are, they are afraid of her," they would say. Even Dimitov, when he saw her from afar, blinked his eyes and signaled to me: "She's the most fearsome one on this planet."

---

[42] From the poem "Remember the Jungle" of Thế Lữ, a famous poet in the 1930s.

I had been warned, so I did not dare underestimate her. This was a woman of around sixty; her hair was turning gray, with one eye already gone bad. Her make-up was done in a way that would make her look a bit more Western, but her teeth were dyed black. As she sat casually chewing betel nuts, she kept a keen eye on the exchanges between Dimitov and Ái and Tích. Her air of casualness was frightening. Although Dimitov was talking to Ái, every now and then he would glance in her direction like an eagle flying above a group of newborn chicks, still alert for the sharp beak of the mother hen.

After having chosen his words carefully, he said:

"It's not that my friend is a bad person. Actually, he's a quite decent man, except for his drinking habit, but what soldier doesn't have that problem, huh? My friend told me that he would stop. If you forgive him, he'll think of something to make it up to you. Please don't leave so soon. Can you stay here for another ten days, until the next salary?"

Ái looked at Madame Sergeant, "What do you think I should tell him? He only has eighteen piastres, and I wanted ... "

"Is he a jealous type?" The old *dame* asked the younger girl.

"I don't know ... No, not normally. Just like anyone else, I think."

Madame Tứ turned to Dimitov:

"*Alo điếc lúy vơ nia đô nê xanh biệt! La bơ tít đoa bẩy dề pho băng xương ăng co đít dua. Xăng qua en đoa bờ lắc kê bua Hanoi búit cơ y a cảm soóc giăng đờ măng đê xa manh.*"[43] [All right, tell him to come and give [her] five piastres. The little one needs to pay her rent for ten more days. If not, she will have to go to Hanoi because there's a sergeant who wants to marry her.]

Dimitov frowned, bit his lips, but did not say anything. In the end, he shook our hands. And still not saying a word, he left. Madame Tứ's eyes trailed him:

"If they want something, they have to have money. If he wants us to wait for ten days, that's five piastres. But if they don't want to pay, then they can just go without it for a month. There's no way we would give in."

So, I see. The house by the Hoa Waterfall was an important place for a certain Russian fellow to try to reestablish the bilateral relation between Viet Nam and some European nation. (Unfortunately, the one hundred years of partnership[44] have to be temporarily suspended due to lack of financial support!)

"Tích! What happened? How come your affair only lasted a few days?"

Miss Tích was too embarrassed to answer. I was surprised at the young girl in a gossamer dress, velvet shoes. I then imagined how the commander-in-chief Doumer[45] felt when a bullet struck him: "Could that be possible?" Tích didn't seem to have mastered the trade.

I had some idea of what kind of person she was, but Madame Corporal made it even clearer:

---

[43] *Alors, dites lui venir donner cinq piastres. La petite doit payer pour pension encore dix jours. Sans quoi elle doit plaquer pour Hanoi puisque il y a quel sergent demander sa main. [Alors, dites-lui de venir payer cinq piastres. La petite doit encore payer dix jours de pension. Sinon, elle doit partir pour Hanoi parce qu'il y a un sergent qui a demandé sa main.]*

[44] Vietnamese expression for a lifelong commitment or partnership, one hundred years of happiness.

[45] Paul Doumer, the governor general of Indochina from 1897-1902. He was the thirteenth president of the French Third Republic and was assassinated in Paris in 1932.

"You see, who would be so stupid? She sold her ring to pay the rent so they could stay together for a few days. Now, that did not get anywhere, and there went the ring!"

Tích timidly said, "I couldn't believe it would happen like that."

"Did you dump him or did he dump you?"

"If he didn't dump me then sooner or later I would dump him. I didn't think you'd know."

"What? An old maid like me? Wouldn't know?" Madame Sergeant interrupted. "I feel so frustrated when I think of you young girls. You had an education and still look at what happened!"

I took the opportunity to ask about the good old days of the two misses, Ái and Tích. From one story to another, and thanks to Madame Sergeant's contemptuous attitude toward life—she couldn't care less about covering up anything—I got a good idea of the melodrama.

Ái and Tích were best of friends. Poverty bound them together, and they loved each other like sisters. It was not clear where they went to school, but they had to quit and started working at a clothing store in Hanoi. They worked ten hours a day for a French lady owner, and their monthly compensation was merely six piastres!

Both endured hardship, and they would have been quite content with what they had if nothing happened. But one can be sure that, in life, something always happens so that one's fate changes; from feeling content to undergoing trying times or from having difficulties to experiencing even more hardship.

Tích was not very educated, so the French lady boss granted her a fair share of ugly names. Ái was smarter and prettier than her friend, so the lady boss was fond of her. And if the missus was fond of her, the master was even more appreciative. That was how the trouble got started.

One day, when the lady boss was not at home, the boss took Ái's hand and pulled her into the bedroom. Next day, she was kicked out of the house. And out went Tích.

"I felt like a precious gem with flaws, so I don't dare to think about getting married to a decent husband. Once a girl is fallen, whether it's her fault or someone else's, she will stay down forever. Don't you agree, Mister? How could I marry an Annamite? If I marry someone nice, then I will bring shame to him and his family, and I don't want to marry some good-for-nothing. So, we came here."

I wasn't sure if I understood everything that Ái had just said. It was quite noble for Ái to think like that. But what about Tích? What had she done to throw her life away? I asked:

"Is your love life also broken up [Did you lose your virginity?], Miss Tích?"

Everyone was looking at Tích, signaling her to answer that question herself. I had to show my concern, and so then she hesitated for a while before speaking up. But when she did, she didn't talk to me directly. She looked at Madame Sergeant:

"You've always said that I am silly and stupid, but it is not true. I'd like to take this opportunity to tell you everything; otherwise you would keep feeling bad for me. I've been having a lover in Hanoi for two years now."

"Ah ha!" Madame Sergeant chimed. Ái continued for her friend,

"They loved each other very much. It was a true, honorable love, Mister. He's a businessman, but he's already married. I told her not to be involved with someone like that, and she would listen to me for a while. Then, I don't know what happened, but they got involved again. One day, she told me she would like to be his second wife. Love always makes people lose their heads! Then a few days later, I heard that things didn't work out because he and the wife had a fight or something like that. See, that's what you get for getting trapped in the love net. Just about that time, when that incident happened to me, she stopped the affair. We were searching for jobs for a long time, but couldn't find anything. The burden of the family was heavy, so we had to listen to those old *dames* in the East Gate area and come here. Tích is much better than me, Mister. She would never have cause for regret. Before entering this lifestyle, she did exactly what Kiều did.[46]

"Second peach is saved for the true love."

Tích's face was red, but she managed to ask me: "Don't you think so, Mister? What is greater than love for each other? Actually, I should be praised."

I wanted to compliment her, but Madame Sergeant beat me to it:

"That's the way to do it! Every time I thought of you losing your virginity to him and letting him rip you off, I just couldn't sit still."

She grinned, showing her teeth as she spoke, and then she reached out for a bamboo stick and whapped it on the bed at the end of her sentence. We thought we were listening to a drum roll at the imperial court and could not contain our laughter. Madame Sergeant continued:

"Now then, what's done is done. We can't cry over spilled milk, and it's no use to regret. But just imagine what it would be like if Tích were still a virgin! A virgin in my hands, that'll be at least thirty piastres in tips. For a legionnaire, getting a virgin is better than having gold. This kind of marriage will always last longer, unless the woman turns tricks or the husband finishes his term and is transferred to another camp."

Ái and Tích complained:

"The life of marrying the Europeans is pathetic, Madame Sergeant. They get drunk, they pick fights, and you never know when they are going to kill us with one of their punches. Tell me, Madame, did anyone ever kill any one of us?"

Madame Sergeant went wild ... Hey, who told you to mess around with the lioness? She screamed:

"What are you afraid of? Unless they catch you sleeping with someone else. What's right is right. If you are right and they are wrong, then scream at them; if they curse at you, then curse back. Do you know what kind of old girl I am? One time, somebody hit me once; I slapped him back three times. Once, someone raised a knife at me, and I pulled up my brassiere. None of them would dare mess with me, you know."

She lowered her voice as she turned to me:

"It's good that they don't usually hit a woman. If they did, it'd be to scare you. But if they really wanted to, one punch and you would hit the dust."

She smiled and continued:

"You have to be smart, especially when you catch them with another woman. You have to act like you're someone important. So if you ever catch them in the act, you don't need to wait for any explanations, just pull on their hair and bite and slap them. Do you think I'm joking, eh? I am not afraid because they rarely hit back. Some guys even like it when you act jealous because he thinks his wife loves him, know what I mean? Where in fact, we're only acting. Who has the energy to be jealous?!"

---

[46] The heroine from Nguyễn Du's *The Tale of Kiều*, which is often considered a nineteenth-century Vietnamese literary masterpiece.

Dimitov will probably return with his friend anytime now. In order to avoid the suspicion that I could be Ái's "husband," Madame Sergeant requests that I leave.

Well, I've had the opportunity to witness the lioness teach her students. And as I was leaving, I was still wondering whether or not Ái and Tích would be good disciples.

8. Sơn Tinh, the Mountain God and Thủy Tinh, the Water God.[47]

Alas, Madame Kiểm Lâm was no Mỵ Nương, the lovely maiden described in Nguyễn Nhược Pháp's poem. Why then were Hector and his soldier buddy—but also his enemy—so willing to risk their names and honor to fight for her and to disgrace each other by calling one another unrecognizable names, the kind that honorable people would not call each other?

Sitting quietly in the corner, with my arms crossed, I was clear out of their sight. The two were busy trying to outdo each other for their "Mỵ Nương." They were too busy trying to outdo each other, so that neither bothered to suspect whether or not I was Madame Kiểm Lâm's lover. In any case, this was not the first time that Hector had met me.

The first time, in this very house, when he came to give his golden heart to Madame Kiểm Lâm, I had had the opportunity to have quite a good chat with the fellow. When he found out that I was a reporter for a Vietnamese newspaper, he politely returned my press card. He immediately asked me about the assassination of Barthou and King Alexander the Third in Marseilles and how this event had created a commotion for the current French government. I gave him the basic summary that I had gathered from the news agency ARIP. I then left him and his lover alone to chat for hours. He also welcomed my investigation of the issue concerning Eurasian children. He fiercely accused legionnaires of gross indifference toward them, and since he was not married, I found that his accusation was quite sincere. I had already escaped his suspicion with relative ease, so this time I wasn't too worried about being at Madame Kiểm Lâm's house. Actually, I was more worried about his enemy. But the two were too busy arguing and paid no attention to me.

In the verbal battle, both sides used rather bad French. I had to listen for a while, and I was surprised when I finally figured out that it was Madame Kiểm Lâm who had chosen the groom, and thus, he became Hector's enemy. He was an older legionnaire, but Hector called him "a camel"[48] out of disrespect. Worse yet, the winning camel was also a dirty Jew [*sale juif*].

Watching the battle between the mountain and water Gods, the princess Mỵ Nương remained very calm and emotionless. She seemed to possess that "*măng phú tú*" [*m'enfous tout*], the I-could-care-less attitude, just like the King Hùng Vương: money received, goods changed hands.

In the beginning, Hector still managed to be polite:

---

[47] According to a famous ancient Vietnamese tale, King Hùng promised to give the hand of his beautiful daughter Mỵ Nương to whomever arrived with the dowry first. Both Sơn Tinh, the mountain god, and Thủy Tinh, the water god, were in the contest. Sơn Tinh arrived earlier and thus got the bride. Thủy Tinh raised the water level to fight back against Sơn Tinh. Sơn Tinh then raised his mountains, so Thủy Tinh was never able to have Mỵ Nương.

[48] A camel (*chameau*) is a slang term for a bastard.

"Allow me to be surprised because I came here and chatted with this woman one week before you did. This very woman also promised her hand to me ... but now this?"

The older legionnaire was frowning. He was trying to smile. Dear Readers, you probably have seen his type before: a rough and unshaven face, pale as a sheet, with huge and dark bags under his eyes, colorless lips, and rotten teeth. A sad-looking type of face when he is expressionless, and a grumpy one when he really wants to smile.

"No, no! It was just five days since I was here last, and this woman also promised to marry me. By the way, how come I never saw you whenever I came here? I think you'd better go. This woman just received ten piastres from me."

Hector painfully turned to Madame Kiểm Lâm:

"So, what have you got to say about your promise?"

Madame Kiểm Lâm answered pathetically:

"*Xê ba ma phốt, nét si bá? Uây, moa bơ rô mét a vu tú đơ, mê luy viêng a văng vu ê a lo xê mông ma ghi! Vu dêt dơn ê bô cú gia lu, moa ba ú lòa!*" [It's not my fault, is it? Sure, I promised both of you, but he came here first, so then he's my husband. You are young and very jealous. I don't like it.][49]

Hector spit on the ground with disgust. He took out a cigarette and turned to his enemy:

"If you steal her from me, then you are truly a camel."

But the clever "camel" replied:

"How could I steal her from you? This is the first time I am meeting you. You're still young and still very naive."

And still very angry, Hector said sarcastically:

"That's right. I am still very young, so I haven't experienced life, unlike you. Especially, I am not a citizen of Austria, so I wouldn't know what the city of love is like.[50] This is the first time I have learned how to be jealous."

This time the "camel" could no longer hold his temper:

"Damn you! You think in my country I am so used to having women cheat on me that I have to come here and hang on to whomever I can find? You're wrong! I take up a woman like I hire a servant. Not this guy, oh no, I am not the type who would let a woman make me suffer!"

Guess the old soldier couldn't care less how the Missus felt. There was nothing he could say, so Hector took out his wallet and threw a note on the table. He looked at both of them:

"All right! Would the couple please calculate the bill? I've come here several times, and every time you'd always invite me to coffee. So this time, I'd like to pay. Here's a piastre." He picked up his hat and headed to the door. Not only did he not bother to shake hands with anyone, he turned his head and said:

"I wish you all the happiness. Oh, by the way, I'd like to introduce you to that young Annamite fellow sitting over there. He's a reporter, and I am sure he'll write up something good about your wonderful love story."

---

[49] *C'est ne pas ma faute, n'est ce pas? Ouais, moi promettre à vous tous deux, mais lui vient avant vous et alors c'est mon mari! Vous êtes jeune et beaucoup jaloux, moi pas vouloir! [Ce n'est pas de ma faute, n'est-ce pas? Ouais, je vous avais fait une promesse à tous les deux, mais il est venu avant vous, et donc, c'est lui mon mari. Vous êtes jeune et très jaloux, et moi je n'aime pas ça.]*

[50] Hector's enemy is from Vienna, which was known as "the city of love" (*Ville d'Amour*).

I had wanted to leave for sometime now, but I just got stuck here.

* * *

I don't know if the old legionnaire paid any attention to Hector's ridicule or not, but he asked my permission to take off his military jacket and invited me to stay for a chat, and said that we should "break the crust of the bread" [*casse croûte*] before engaging ourselves in conversation. Hector's cynical introduction left me no choice but to accept eagerly. I figured if the old legionnaire was up to something, then I would deal with it as it came.

After Madame Kiểm Lâm ordered one of her kids to buy some bread, she lit an oil lamp, took out a tin of butter, a few eggs, and several links of sausages, and started preparing the food. From this time, the three of us chatted very warmly, and thanks to the good fragrance of the food and wine, the conversation wasn't too … tasteless.

"Because I dished out the money first, I now have a wife. Don't you think this sort of marriage is more like a business transaction?"

I had to "roll my tongue seven times" before I could answer:

"If you say that, then in my country since the beginning of time, all marriages are business transactions. As you probably already know, the majority of the people in my country still follow the old customs. There aren't many people who are able to marry the ones they love. It never happens in my society that a young couple is able to discuss their affairs freely with one another. So receiving offerings from a man is no different than a business transaction. The ten piastres that you gave her, according to our marriage customs, I would consider that as a form of a dowry from the groom's family. That's all. Life is very simple. Please don't worry that I laugh at you because if I did so, I would have to laugh at my country first."

That was all I said, but the old man seemed to enjoy it immensely. His gray head kept bobbing up and down in agreement. This old soldier never knew that his neck was playing an honorable role, just like the neck of an Annamite congressman.

To be honest, I was being quite … clever. I continued:

"I have read quite a bit about marriages, and I feel bitterly torn. For example, this Western philosopher, well, unfortunately, I can't recall his name (well, how could I really since I am making this up?). This fellow, he wrote something like this: 'What is there to detest in prostitution? Why does every society hold prostitution in condemnation?'

"If you really think about it, say if you marry a nice girl from a good family, we men have to spend hundreds or thousands of piastres on her. They [these women] allow us to spend this enormous sum, so obviously they will have to spend the rest of their lives with us. So if you're talking about 'the affair of a hundred years,' you'd have to be willing to spend a big sum. On the other hand, when we go visit a prostitute for a night, we lose only a small amount of money. Whether one is her lover for one night or for the rest of her life, all women are still prostitutes. Therefore, it makes no sense when a 'life-term prostitute' looks down on the one-night ones: just because she [the 'life-term prostitute'] has more experience? Don't you see? All human beings are like that. We all think badly of each other. Regardless whether we are from the East or from the West, from an advanced or a barbaric nation, you are just like me, and I am just like you; why should we be worried by what other people think?"

Lord! I thought the old soldier had gone mad! He grabbed my hands and shook them up and down, making my body swing from one side to the other.

The wife had finished preparing dinner. The kid from her previous husband also brought some bread home. We dutifully went to the table. Ah, Dear Readers, when you read these lines, don't you start thinking that I had fabricated the above story in order to get food. I was just being a smart aleck. Furthermore, I couldn't let Hector do that to us.

The new groom revealed his true happiness:

"Dear Mister, what I like best about my wife is that I can trust her. Two fellows wanted to marry her: one is old and weak, and the other is young and strong; she chose the older one, me. That's enough to make me feel content that I have a faithful wife."

His statement reminded me of what Madame Kiểm had said earlier about Hector's jealous nature. This was what I got when I asked her later:

"Well, the first time he met you, he was very nice and welcoming, don't you think so? But the second time he saw you, he was very inquisitive about you. I had to explain to him in great detail over and over. I told him it was very unlikely that a person like me would get involved with someone who is as young as you. Even he himself has said: 'Right, an educated person, someone who's from a high-class (?)[51] background would be too cautious to be in this area, let alone to go look for a no-good woman, and so on.' I thought he had understood. But the second time, he made me tell him if you were still here or had left for Hanoi. In the end, I couldn't take it anymore, I told him straight out: 'Hey, if you want to marry me, you come here. I am not begging you; so don't ask too many questions. Don't be ridiculously jealous.'"

"Why did you accept the proposal from both of them?" I asked.

She laughed and replied nonchalantly: "Why not?"

I can't believe that in the business of marrying Europeans people don't even bother to save their reputations like some people cover up dirt with a shiny coat of paint. It's just a buying and selling world, and it all has to do with the right price.

She continued, "Those times when he came to haggle over the price, I did tell him I would marry him only if no one gave me the money first."

* * *

One could say that at this moment, the life of Madame Kiểm could be considered happy and peaceful. While she was doing the dishes and resuming the title of a "domestic general," her new groom called out to the three kids from her previous two husbands. He brought the youngest to his lap and lovingly kissed the child.

Was Madame Kiểm happy? I couldn't really tell. Her face was still calm and emotionless, like a stone, and cold like a piece of metal. This was a wedding night, and this woman showed no sign of emotion. How strange and how unlovable! Then suddenly I remembered that she had had the same emotionless expression when a German soldier hit her. Nothing has changed.

---

[51] The question mark is inserted in the original text by the author to illustrate his reaction to the speaker's assumption that he is from a "high-class" background.

I stood up and shook the husband's hand. To the wife I said:

"Well, please excuse me, missus. I must go. I wish the bride and the groom a hundred years of happiness."

She smiled as she replied:

"Well, if we get along well, three years at most. At the end of three years, if he gets transferred, I will take another step."

9. MONOPOLY IDEOLOGY

I had been walking around for four days now, and I had gathered quite enough materials, so it's time for me to return to Hanoi. I also wanted to go to the Thông Pagoda district. I had had an opportunity to witness a "divorce" and a "wedding" of Madame Kiểm Lâm. I had had a heart-to-heart chat with Suzanne; I had listened to the stories of the nine wives of Dimitov and seen Madame Sergeant Tứ, the founding mother of the *dames*, the dethroned lioness, teaching the later generations the *"Tuých"* [*truc*], the tricks of the trade. My only wish now is to meet Madame Ách Nhoáng to collect some more "samples," and that would nearly complete the collection of stories about this industry.

Unfortunately, the beverage-stand lady, the person who had introduced me to Dimitov, informed me that Madame Ách Nhoáng was not in a good mood. She had been having a row with a vegetable seller, and her mood could be best described as like the Mandarin Khâm's. The mandarin's precious ears were disturbed because the villagers could not stop the frogs from croaking. He ordered his general to kill the entire village. I was in the market, but the timing was not right, so I had no choice but to return to the Cổ Mễ village to say good-bye to my friend before going out to the train station. Still, I did manage to get some tidbits about the fallen "ex-queen." In the good old days, she used to scream out fire in Việt Trì, her territory. Then the law of compensation took over; she became just a poor plain woman and had no choice but to leave those glorious times behind.

But the devil must have been on my side. By the time I got to the Alamba cinema, and as I was trying to figure out which train to take to Hanoi, I ran into Hector, the water god. I am sure you readers haven't forgotten about the tragic love affair of this legionnaire. He pulled my arm and excitedly told me that he had found someone new, and this new French-Annamite "fiancée" was much prettier than the despicable Madame Kiểm Lâm. He asked me if I wanted to see what she looked like. Naturally, I didn't refuse.

That is the reason why I had said the devil must have been on my side. I ended up witnessing a horrifying scene, a scene that could send me to the ancient times, the time when a human's life was as valuable as a worm's, the time when a local mandarin was as cruel as the Ngọa Triều Emperor. Even now, as I am sitting here underneath a lamp writing this reportage, I still feel angered by it, and the injustice still makes my blood boil.

When we arrived at his "fiancée's" house, it was already dark. From several steps beyond the gate, we could hear the noise of someone crying, and we were surprised because it did not sound like a child's cry. What's more, the cry was fused with the whoosh sounds of a rattan whip.

Hector and I tiptoed forward and pressed our noses against a crack of the door. On top of a Western bed lay the ivory-skinned, heavenly white, stripped-naked body of a young woman on a colorful rattan mat. Her face was buried in a pillow, and her "peaches" writhed under the whip of Madame Ách Nhoáng. Madame Ách Nhoáng was quite methodical about her whipping. She would hold her hands up high and bring the whip down, casually—but without cruelty—and slowly, like an old villager clumsily pounding the village drum. So, it seemed that the Madame was in the middle of educating her only daughter.

After having seen the heavenly body squirming no less than three times, Hector slammed the door open. He looked around the room, hands in his pockets, and entered the house.

"Oh, my God! They have arrived."

At that moment, I couldn't tell whether Hector was feeling pain or contempt. He just bit his lips and stared into space. In the house, the beating and the crying had stopped. There were only the sounds of shoes and wooden clogs shuffling like mad. Hector signaled me to enter the house. I tipped my hat to Madame Ách, but she looked at her daughter:

"Don't know what's gotten into you to say that I've gone mad!"

Then she threw the whip into the corner of the room and flopped herself in a hammock. She couldn't be bothered talking to Hector or me. She just sat there and looked into the distance.

Was this some smart woman who had gone mad or some lunatic who was smart? Her behavior prompted me to think that the cruel beating session was just a front. Who really knew what her intentions were: an opportunity to expose the intimate details of her daughter's lovely body? As I was busy with my thoughts, the daughter reappeared from the room next door. Her luscious body had been covered; her dark eyes were dried of tears. Seeing her still embarrassed, Hector quickly introduced us:

"Here, this is somebody I just met. He's a newspaper reporter. What your mother did, I am sure that anyone, not only a newspaperman, would say is barbaric."

He turned to me:

"I can't believe your people would do that to each other. This is no different than those barbarians in Africa."

The daughter quickly asked me and her ally to sit down:

"Mister, please don't laugh at my mother," she said. "She's gone mad. If I hadn't let her beat me, she would have broken many things in the house. We just can't afford to keep on replacing things whenever her madness strikes."

Then she used French to explain to her "fiancé" what she had just said. Her French was rather fluent, not too bad at all. As for the fellow, his sense of compassion had been stirred up. He felt that his life would now have a purpose, if he could be her partner in life to protect her heavenly body from her deranged mother. He pulled her to him:

"Oh, my love. How much do I really love you."

Finally, being stupid, Hector pulled her closer and kissed her nonstop. Dear Readers, I called him stupid, not because he wasn't being discreet in front of a stranger. But, just like me, he was a member of the audience who had just experienced a performance in which his lover's clothes were completely stripped off. The image of that scene had not left me; can you see that the couple's caressing was no less than a dirty picture show? So if I stirred up any not-so-clean thoughts, Dear Readers, please understand it was not my fault. But I wasn't stupid enough to let people carry out their acts of affection openly in front of me. Me, myself, I don't even know where I will be sleeping and who I will be sleeping with tonight ...

Madame Ách Nhoáng had disappeared, but her daughter definitely knew the reason why her mother occasionally had a fit.

"Mister, my mother has had a miserable life. When she was young, she was quite well off, but she is very poor now. My mother has become mad because of poverty. The reason she is hard on me is because she's seen the way mixed-blood children treat their mothers. My fate is doomed, all because of them!"

"What I'd like to know is, when your mother was still living in Việt Trì, what got into her to think that she could keep a monopoly on the industry? According to many people, no one who moved there could ever find a husband."

The daughter was glad to explain:

"That's a good question. My mother wasn't as mean as what they thought. It's all because of that industry (dear, that word again) of marrying the Europeans. This occupation has a lot of twists and turns. A lot of women don't have a bit of integrity when they enter this profession. They don't know how to evaluate the market; they get married with whomever and regardless of how much money is involved. Then they badmouth, get jealous of, and compete against each other, and then the prices go down. For example, say you have set a price, and all of a sudden, someone from who-knows-where jumps in carrying a 'sale' sign, wouldn't you be angry too?"

I just smiled. She was so excited. She continued,

"They are so low class, those women! Some of them think that my mother is being punished because now she's poor, and they are getting back at her by speaking ill of her. Isn't life pathetic?"

My dear lass, I think you've lied to me! I respect her for being loyal to her mother, but Madame Ách Nhoáng's wanting to set a high standard for "the industry" was only a fraction of the problem. It was her habit of her bribe-taking from other *dames* that made up for the rest.

About eight years ago, whoever wanted to find a husband in Việt Trì had to pay her respects to Madame Ách Nhoáng. If they didn't, they wouldn't be staying there for very long. Even those *dames* who followed their husbands to relocate in the area would still be under Madame Ách's domain. No one knew for sure what her "*tuých*" [*truc*—tricks] were. However, there was still that law of compensation.

One day, Madame Ách met one of the *dames* who had followed her husband François to resettle up there.

"Hey, you're married only to a corporal," Madame Ách Nhoáng continued, "but it doesn't matter if your husband is a sergeant, or a sergeant-major, if you are going to live in this area, you have to know who I am!" Madame Ách started to raise her voice.

Madame Corporal François immediately spoke up:

"Dear sister, I am very aware of who you are. But having just moved to the area, I am yet to be settled to come and pay you my respects. Do forgive me."

Madame Ách was somewhat satisfied. Only somewhat satisfied. Because Madam Corporal François arrived empty handed. Not only that, her hands were positioned in the back, her "*derriere*"—how disrespectful! When she saw there wasn't going to be any "humble" gift offered, Madame Ách yelled:

"Who's stopping you from coming here and paying respect! You have to know the right things to do. You still have to know who I am. Do you want to stay here or what?"

"Hey, this girl is telling the truth. This girl only wants to leave," answered Madame Corporal François. Then, she moved forward, raising a rather ... large hammer over her head.

One pound. The golden throne was crumbled. Madame Ách Nhoáng had become a dethroned queen.

I envision an enormous woman sitting next to a perfumed letterbox, her face as big as its lid, giving orders to other *dames*. Now, I see only a woman whose meaty body is cramped in a short-sleeved, flowered blouse and whose remaining power is to strip the clothes off her daughter to cane her.

* * *

"Are you happy now?" I asked.

Hector looked at me puzzled, "What do you mean?"

"Happiness is when you are able to have compassion for others, especially when your feeling leads to love. Happiness is when you love someone and that person loves you back."

Hector stood up and shook my hand:

"If that's what happiness is, then I am very happy. I'd like to inform you that my fiancée is now my wife. Tonight is our wedding night."

I was shocked, "So quickly? How did you do it?"

"When I saw how mean her mother was to her, I was determined to marry her."

I was almost moved by that heroic step. I was happy for the woman, a sad and agonized woman. I was happy that she had finally found a friend for life. I respected the soldier for having a kind heart, a heart that knew what human compassion was. I was still dreaming ... that the woman didn't get married because of money and Hector didn't fork up the dough to buy physical pleasure. During the course of my investigation, this was probably the only couple that got married for love.

"Furthermore, today is my payday."

That was the last thing Hector said. Alas! Hector has "crushed" my dream. Hector was truly an idiot, a super idiot!

10. CONCLUSION

In the beginning, I promised my readers that I would do a report on the *dames* who are married to the soldiers of the colonial army as well as those who are married to the European civilians. From these reports of the *dames* who married the legionnaires, I think the readers can imagine the peculiarities that come with the industry of marrying the Europeans. Still, I would like to go investigate those "high-class" *dames* as well.

The encouragement from my colleagues has made me extremely happy. However, I am aware that not everyone is fond of this reportage. We received three letters that made the editor-in-chief, Mr. Đỗ Văn, scratch his forehead.

One of the letters was from some nameless *dame*. She encouraged me and also promised to provide me with some "fascinating" stories. That doesn't count. The second one was from a Frenchman. He was extremely encouraging. He urged the author to go quickly find those powerful *dames*, those who are married to plantation managers, businessmen, etc. His enthusiasm was rather suspicious; it might incite me to get into trouble.

The third was also from a Frenchman. He calmly forewarned us of the kind of lawsuits that my newspaper would encounter if they continued to print my reportage. He stated that I could not proclaim that the Europeans and the Orientals would never be in harmony, that I should not plant doubts in the Westerners' minds, and that I had no right to destroy many wonderful Franco-Annamite unions by insinuating that when Westerners marry their local wives, for them it is like buying a piece of merchandise. Pretty soon I will not have the freedom to continue to cajole and humiliate people.

Well, perhaps they all make sense.

But, I can see the smiles of the two lawmen.

To be afraid is cowardly. Then again, sometimes it is not. Furthermore, what is the use of saying so much? The truth is always the truth, no?

The power from above would fall on me if I continued.

All right, then. I won't.

REFERENCES

ENGLISH-LANGUAGE REFERENCES

Anderson, Roy C. *Devils, Not Men: The History of the French Foreign Legion*. London: Robert Dale, 1987.

Bloom, Edward A. and Lillian D. Bloom, *Satire's Persuasive Voice*. Ithaca and London: Cornell University Press, 1979.

Feinberg, Leonard. *Introduction to Satire*. Ames, IA: The Iowa State University Press, 1967.

Geraghty, Tony. *March or Die: France and the Foreign Legion*. London: Grafton, 1986.

Hernández, Guillermo E. *Chicano Satire: A Study in Literary Studies*. Austin, TX: University of Texas Press, 1991.

Hoang Ngoc Thanh. *Vietnam's Social and Political Development as Seen through the Modern Novel*. New York: Peter Lang, 1991.

Jamieson, Neil L. *Understanding Vietnam*. Berkeley, CA: University of California Press, 1995.

Kuester, Martin. *Framing Truths: Parodic Structures in Contemporary English-Canadian Historical Novels*. Toronto: University of Toronto Press, 1992.

Lockhart, Greg, and Monique Lockhart, trans. *The Light of the Capital: Three Modern Vietnamese Classics*. Kuala Lumpur and New York: Oxford University Press, 1996.

Marr, David G. *Vietnamese Tradition on Trial, 1920–1945*. Berkeley, CA: University of California Press, 1981.

Mercer, Charles E. *Legion of Strangers: The Vivid History of a Unique Military Tradition—The French Foreign Legion*. New York, NY: Holt, Rinehart, and Winston, 1986 [1964].

Ngo Vinh Long. *Before the Revolution: The Vietnamese Peasants Under the French*. New York, NY: Columbia University Press, 1974.

Nguyen Dang Liem. "Cases and Verbs in Pidgin French (Tay Boi) in Vietnam." *Journal of Creole Studies* 1 (1977).

Nguyen Dang Liem. "Cases and Verbs in Pidgin French (Tay Boi) in Vietnam." In *Pacific Linguistics Series A*, vol. 57, Papers in Pidgin and Creole Linguistics, no. 2, Canberra: Department of Linguistics, Australian National University, 1979.

Petro, Peter. *Modern Satire: Four Studies*. Berlin, New York, and Amsterdam: Mouton Publishers, 1982.

Purdie, Susan. *Comedy: The Mastery of Discourse*. Toronto: University of Toronto Press, 1993.

Reinecke, E. John. "Tay Boi: Notes on the Pidgin French Spoken in Vietnam." In *Pidginization and Creolization of Languages* (Proceedings of a Conference Held at the University of the West Indies, Mona, Jamaica, April 1968), ed. Dell Hymes. Cambridge: Cambridge University Press, 1971.

Salzmann, Zdenek. *Language, Culture, and Society: An Introduction to Linguistics Anthropology*. Boulder, CO: Westview Press, 1993.

Vasquez, Olga A., Lucinda Pease-Alvarez, and Sheila M. Shannon. *Pushing Boundaries: Language and Culture in a Mexicano Community*. New York, NY: Cambridge University Press, 1994.

Woodside, Alexander. *Community and Revolution in Vietnam*. Boston, MA: Houghton Mifflin, 1976.

Zinoman, Peter, ed. *Dumb Luck* (Số Đỏ), trans. Nguyen Nguyet Cam and Peter Zinoman. Ann Arbor, MI: The University of Michigan Press, 2002.

NON-ENGLISH LANGUAGE REFERENCES:

Lại Nguyên Ân, ed. *Vũ Trọng Phụng: Tài năng và Sự thật* [Vu Trong Phung: The talent and the truth]. Hanoi: NXB Writers' Association Publishing, 1992.

Mai Hương, ed. *Vũ Trọng Phụng: Một tài năng độc đáo. Nhà văn Việt Nam. Tác Phẩm và Dư Luận* [Vu Trong Phung: A rare and unique talent. Vietnamese writers: Works and criticism]. Hanoi: Cultural and Information Publishing, 2000.

Nguyễn Đăng Mạnh, "Introduction." In *Vũ Trọng Phụng: Selected Works*. Hanoi: Văn Học Publishing, 1987.

Nguyễn Hoành Khung and Lại Nguyên Ân, eds., *Vũ Trọng Phụng: Con Người và tác phẩm* [Vu Trong Phung: The man and his works]. Hanoi: Writers' Association Publishing, 1992.

Phan Thế Hồng and Janine Gillon, trans. *Le Fabuleux Destin De Xuan Le Rouquin* [Số Đỏ]. Hanoi: World Publishing, 1998.

Tâm Lang. *Tôi Kéo Xe*. Los Amitos, CA: Xuân Thu, 1988.

Trần Hữu Tạ, ed. *Vũ Trọng Phụng: Hôm qua và Hôm nay* [Vu Trong Phung: Yesterday and today]. Ho Chi Minh City: Ho Chi Minh City Publishing, 1992.

Trần Hữu Tạ, ed. *Vũ Trọng Phụng: Những tác phẩm tiêu biểu* [Vu Trong Phung's notable works]. Ho Chi Minh City: The Ministry of Education and Training, Education Publishing, 2000.

WORKS BY VŨ TRỌNG PHỤNG:

A bibliography of Phụng's work may be found in Trần Hữu Tạ, ed. *Vũ Trọng Phụng: Những tác phẩm tiêu biểu* [Vu Trong Phung's notable works].

An additional body of work by Vũ Trọng Phụng was discovered and has been published in *Vũ Trọng Phụng. Chống Nạng Lên Đường: Chùm sáng tác đầu tay mới tìm thấy năm 2000.* [Walking with crutches: Works newly found in the year of 2000]. Hanoi: Writers' Association Publishing, 2001.

Reportage:
Kỹ Nghệ Lấy Tây [The industry of marrying Europeans]. Hanoi: Phương Đông, 1934.
Cạm Bẫy Người [How to trap people]. Hanoi: Văn Học Publishing, 1993 [1933].
Cơm Thầy Cơm Cô [Under someone else's roof]. Hanoi: Minh Phương, 1937 [1936].
Lục Xì [The VD clinic]. Hanoi: Minh Phương, 1937.

Short Stories:

"Chống Nạng Lên Đường" [Walking on crutches]
"Bộ Răng Vàng" [Golden dentures]
"Một Đồng Bạc" [One piaster]
"Gương Tống Tiền" [A model blackmail]
"Người Có Quyền" [Powerful people]
"Tết Ăn Mày" [Beggar's new year]

Lê thị Đức Hạnh and Xuân Tùng, eds. *Vũ Trọng Phụng: Selected Short Stories*. Hanoi: Writers' Association Publishing, 1996.

Plays:

"Không Một Tiếng Vang" [Not one sound]
"Tài tử" [Movie stars]
"Chín Đầu Một Lúc" [Nine heads at once]
"Cái chết bí mật của người trúng số độc đắc" [The mysterious death of the lottery winner]

Novels:

Giông Tố [The storm]. Hanoi: Văn Học Publishing, 1996 [1936].
Làm Đĩ [Prostitution]. Hanoi: Văn Học Publishing, 1996 [1937].
Số Đỏ [Lucky destiny]. Hanoi: Văn Học Publishing, 1990 [1936].
Vỡ Đê [Broken dikes]. In *Vũ Trọng Phụng Selected Works*. Hanoi: Văn Học Publishing, 1993 [1936].

Films:

Giông Tố. [Vietnam]. Westminster, CA: Viet Press; Little Saigon Video, 1991.
Số Đỏ. [Vietnam]. Fountain Valley, CA: Viet Press; Little Saigon Video, 1990.

SOUTHEAST ASIA PROGRAM PUBLICATIONS
Cornell University

Studies on Southeast Asia

Number 39   *The Indonesian Supreme Court: A Study of Institutional Collapse,*
Sebastiaan Pompe. 2005. 494 pp. ISBN 0-877277-38-9 (pb).

Number 38   *Spirited Politics: Religion and Public Life in Contemporary Southeast Asia,*
ed. Andrew C. Willford and Kenneth M. George. 2005. 210 pp.
ISBN 0-87727-737-0.

Number 37   *Sumatran Sultanate and Colonial State: Jambi and the Rise of Dutch
Imperialism, 1830-1907,* Elsbeth Locher-Scholten, trans. Beverley
Jackson. 2004. 332 pp. ISBN 0-87727-736-2.

Number 36   *Southeast Asia over Three Generations: Essays Presented to Benedict R. O'G.
Anderson,* ed. James T. Siegel and Audrey R. Kahin. 2003. 398 pp. ISBN
0-87727-735-4.

Number 35   *Nationalism and Revolution in Indonesia,* George McTurnan Kahin, intro.
Benedict R. O'G. Anderson (reprinted from 1952 edition, Cornell
University Press, with permission). 2003. 530 pp. ISBN 0-87727-734-6.

Number 34   *Golddiggers, Farmers, and Traders in the "Chinese Districts" of West
Kalimantan, Indonesia,* Mary Somers Heidhues. 2003. 316 pp.
ISBN 0-87727-733-8.

Number 33   *Opusculum de Sectis apud Sinenses et Tunkinenses (A Small Treatise on the
Sects among the Chinese and Tonkinese): A Study of Religion in China and
North Vietnam in the Eighteenth Century,* Father Adriano de St. Thecla,
trans. Olga Dror, with Mariya Berezovska. 2002. 363 pp.
ISBN 0-87727-732-X.

Number 32   *Fear and Sanctuary: Burmese Refugees in Thailand,* Hazel J. Lang. 2002.
204 pp. ISBN 0-87727-731-1.

Number 31   *Modern Dreams: An Inquiry into Power, Cultural Production, and the
Cityscape in Contemporary Urban Penang, Malaysia,* Beng-Lan Goh. 2002.
225 pp. ISBN 0-87727-730-3.

Number 30   *Violence and the State in Suharto's Indonesia,* ed. Benedict R. O'G.
Anderson. 2001. Second printing, 2002. 247 pp. ISBN 0-87727-729-X.

Number 29   *Studies in Southeast Asian Art: Essays in Honor of Stanley J. O'Connor,* ed.
Nora A. Taylor. 2000. 243 pp. Illustrations. ISBN 0-87727-728-1.

Number 28   *The Hadrami Awakening: Community and Identity in the Netherlands East
Indies, 1900-1942,* Natalie Mobini-Kesheh. 1999. 174 pp.
ISBN 0-87727-727-3.

Number 27   *Tales from Djakarta: Caricatures of Circumstances and their Human Beings,*
Pramoedya Ananta Toer. 1999. 145 pp. ISBN 0-87727-726-5.

Number 26   *History, Culture, and Region in Southeast Asian Perspectives,* rev. ed., O.
W. Wolters. 1999. Second printing, 2004. 275 pp. ISBN 0-87727-725-7.

Number 25   *Figures of Criminality in Indonesia, the Philippines, and Colonial Vietnam,*
ed. Vicente L. Rafael. 1999. 259 pp. ISBN 0-87727-724-9.

Number 24   *Paths to Conflagration: Fifty Years of Diplomacy and Warfare in Laos,
Thailand, and Vietnam, 1778-1828,* Mayoury Ngaosyvathn and
Pheuiphanh Ngaosyvathn. 1998. 268 pp. ISBN 0-87727-723-0.

Number 23   *Nguyễn Cochinchina: Southern Vietnam in the Seventeenth and Eighteenth Centuries*, Li Tana. 1998. Second printing, 2002. 194 pp. ISBN 0-87727-722-2.

Number 22   *Young Heroes: The Indonesian Family in Politics*, Saya S. Shiraishi. 1997. 183 pp. ISBN 0-87727-721-4.

Number 21   *Interpreting Development: Capitalism, Democracy, and the Middle Class in Thailand*, John Girling. 1996. 95 pp. ISBN 0-87727-720-6.

Number 20   *Making Indonesia*, ed. Daniel S. Lev, Ruth McVey. 1996. 201 pp. ISBN 0-87727-719-2.

Number 19   *Essays into Vietnamese Pasts*, ed. K. W. Taylor, John K. Whitmore. 1995. 288 pp. ISBN 0-87727-718-4.

Number 18   *In the Land of Lady White Blood: Southern Thailand and the Meaning of History*, Lorraine M. Gesick. 1995. 106 pp. ISBN 0-87727-717-6.

Number 17   *The Vernacular Press and the Emergence of Modern Indonesian Consciousness*, Ahmat Adam. 1995. 220 pp. ISBN 0-87727-716-8.

Number 16   *The Nan Chronicle*, trans., ed. David K. Wyatt. 1994. 158 pp. ISBN 0-87727-715-X.

Number 15   *Selective Judicial Competence: The Cirebon-Priangan Legal Administration, 1680–1792*, Mason C. Hoadley. 1994. 185 pp. ISBN 0-87727-714-1.

Number 14   *Sjahrir: Politics and Exile in Indonesia*, Rudolf Mrázek. 1994. 536 pp. ISBN 0-87727-713-3.

Number 13   *Fair Land Sarawak: Some Recollections of an Expatriate Officer*, Alastair Morrison. 1993. 196 pp. ISBN 0-87727-712-5.

Number 12   *Fields from the Sea: Chinese Junk Trade with Siam during the Late Eighteenth and Early Nineteenth Centuries*, Jennifer Cushman. 1993. 206 pp. ISBN 0-87727-711-7.

Number 11   *Money, Markets, and Trade in Early Southeast Asia: The Development of Indigenous Monetary Systems to AD 1400*, Robert S. Wicks. 1992. 2nd printing 1996. 354 pp., 78 tables, illus., maps. ISBN 0-87727-710-9.

Number 10   *Tai Ahoms and the Stars: Three Ritual Texts to Ward Off Danger*, trans., ed. B. J. Terwiel, Ranoo Wichasin. 1992. 170 pp. ISBN 0-87727-709-5.

Number 9   *Southeast Asian Capitalists*, ed. Ruth McVey. 1992. 2nd printing 1993. 220 pp. ISBN 0-87727-708-7.

Number 8   *The Politics of Colonial Exploitation: Java, the Dutch, and the Cultivation System*, Cornelis Fasseur, ed. R. E. Elson, trans. R. E. Elson, Ary Kraal. 1992. 2nd printing 1994. 266 pp. ISBN 0-87727-707-9.

Number 7   *A Malay Frontier: Unity and Duality in a Sumatran Kingdom*, Jane Drakard. 1990. 2nd printing 2003. 215 pp. ISBN 0-87727-706-0.

Number 6   *Trends in Khmer Art*, Jean Boisselier, ed. Natasha Eilenberg, trans. Natasha Eilenberg, Melvin Elliott. 1989. 124 pp., 24 plates. ISBN 0-87727-705-2.

Number 5   *Southeast Asian Ephemeris: Solar and Planetary Positions, A.D. 638–2000*, J. C. Eade. 1989. 175 pp. ISBN 0-87727-704-4.

Number 3   *Thai Radical Discourse: The Real Face of Thai Feudalism Today*, Craig J. Reynolds. 1987. 2nd printing 1994. 186 pp. ISBN 0-87727-702-8.

Number 1   *The Symbolism of the Stupa*, Adrian Snodgrass. 1985. Revised with
              index, 1988. 3rd printing 1998. 469 pp. ISBN 0-87727-700-1.

SEAP Series

Number 22   *The Industry of Marrying Europeans*, Vũ Trọng Phụng, trans. Thúy
              Tranviet. 2006. 66 pp. ISBN 0-877271-40-2 (pb).

Number 21   *Securing a Place: Small-Scale Artisans in Modern Indonesia*, Elizabeth
              Morrell. 2005. 220 pp. ISBN 0-877271-39-9.

Number 20   *Southern Vietnam under the Reign of Minh Mạng (1820-1841): Central
              Policies and Local Response*, Choi Byung Wook. 2004. 226pp. ISBN 0-0-
              877271-40-2.

Number 19   *Gender, Household, State: Đổi Mới in Việt Nam*, ed. Jayne Werner and
              Danièle Bélanger. 2002. 151 pp. ISBN 0-87727-137-2.

Number 18   *Culture and Power in Traditional Siamese Government*, Neil A. Englehart.
              2001. 130 pp. ISBN 0-87727-135-6.

Number 17   *Gangsters, Democracy, and the State*, ed. Carl A. Trocki. 1998. Second
              printing, 2002. 94 pp. ISBN 0-87727-134-8.

Number 16   *Cutting across the Lands: An Annotated Bibliography on Natural Resource
              Management and Community Development in Indonesia, the Philippines,
              and Malaysia*, ed. Eveline Ferretti. 1997. 329 pp. ISBN 0-87727-133-X.

Number 15   *The Revolution Falters: The Left in Philippine Politics after 1986*, ed.
              Patricio N. Abinales. 1996. Second printing, 2002. 182 pp. ISBN 0-
              87727-132-1.

Number 14   *Being Kammu: My Village, My Life*, Damrong Tayanin. 1994. 138 pp., 22
              tables, illus., maps. ISBN 0-87727-130-5.

Number 13   *The American War in Vietnam*, ed. Jayne Werner, David Hunt. 1993.
              132 pp. ISBN 0-87727-131-3.

Number 12   *The Voice of Young Burma*, Aye Kyaw. 1993. 92 pp. ISBN 0-87727-129-1.

Number 11   *The Political Legacy of Aung San*, ed. Josef Silverstein. Revised edition
              1993. 169 pp. ISBN 0-87727-128-3.

Number 10   *Studies on Vietnamese Language and Literature: A Preliminary
              Bibliography*, Nguyen Dinh Tham. 1992. 227 pp. ISBN 0-87727-127-5.

Number 8   *From PKI to the Comintern, 1924–1941: The Apprenticeship of the Malayan
              Communist Party*, Cheah Boon Kheng. 1992. 147 pp. ISBN 0-87727-125-9.

Number 7   *Intellectual Property and US Relations with Indonesia, Malaysia, Singapore,
              and Thailand*, Elisabeth Uphoff. 1991. 67 pp. ISBN 0-87727-124-0.

Number 6   *The Rise and Fall of the Communist Party of Burma (CPB)*, Bertil Lintner.
              1990. 124 pp. 26 illus., 14 maps. ISBN 0-87727-123-2.

Number 5   *Japanese Relations with Vietnam: 1951–1987*, Masaya Shiraishi. 1990.
              174 pp. ISBN 0-87727-122-4.

Number 3   *Postwar Vietnam: Dilemmas in Socialist Development*, ed. Christine White,
              David Marr. 1988. 2nd printing 1993. 260 pp. ISBN 0-87727-120-8.

Number 2   *The Dobama Movement in Burma (1930–1938)*, Khin Yi. 1988. 160 pp.
              ISBN 0-87727-118-6.

Cornell Modern Indonesia Project Publications

Number 75   *A Tour of Duty: Changing Patterns of Military Politics in Indonesia in the 1990s*. Douglas Kammen and Siddharth Chandra. 1999. 99 pp. ISBN 0-87763-049-6.

Number 74   *The Roots of Acehnese Rebellion 1989–1992*, Tim Kell. 1995. 103 pp. ISBN 0-87763-040-2.

Number 73   *"White Book" on the 1992 General Election in Indonesia*, trans. Dwight King. 1994. 72 pp. ISBN 0-87763-039-9.

Number 72   *Popular Indonesian Literature of the Qur'an*, Howard M. Federspiel. 1994. 170 pp. ISBN 0-87763-038-0.

Number 71   *A Javanese Memoir of Sumatra, 1945–1946: Love and Hatred in the Liberation War*, Takao Fusayama. 1993. 150 pp. ISBN 0-87763-037-2.

Number 70   *East Kalimantan: The Decline of a Commercial Aristocracy*, Burhan Magenda. 1991. 120 pp. ISBN 0-87763-036-4.

Number 69   *The Road to Madiun: The Indonesian Communist Uprising of 1948*, Elizabeth Ann Swift. 1989. 120 pp. ISBN 0-87763-035-6.

Number 68   *Intellectuals and Nationalism in Indonesia: A Study of the Following Recruited by Sutan Sjahrir in Occupation Jakarta*, J. D. Legge. 1988. 159 pp. ISBN 0-87763-034-8.

Number 67   *Indonesia Free: A Biography of Mohammad Hatta*, Mavis Rose. 1987. 252 pp. ISBN 0-87763-033-X.

Number 66   *Prisoners at Kota Cane*, Leon Salim, trans. Audrey Kahin. 1986. 112 pp. ISBN 0-87763-032-1.

Number 65   *The Kenpeitai in Java and Sumatra*, trans. Barbara G. Shimer, Guy Hobbs, intro. Theodore Friend. 1986. 80 pp. ISBN 0-87763-031-3.

Number 64   *Suharto and His Generals: Indonesia's Military Politics, 1975–1983*, David Jenkins. 1984. 4th printing 1997. 300 pp. ISBN 0-87763-030-5.

Number 62   *Interpreting Indonesian Politics: Thirteen Contributions to the Debate, 1964–1981*, ed. Benedict Anderson, Audrey Kahin, intro. Daniel S. Lev. 1982. 3rd printing 1991. 172 pp. ISBN 0-87763-028-3.

Number 60   *The Minangkabau Response to Dutch Colonial Rule in the Nineteenth Century*, Elizabeth E. Graves. 1981. 157 pp. ISBN 0-87763-000-3.

Number 59   *Breaking the Chains of Oppression of the Indonesian People: Defense Statement at His Trial on Charges of Insulting the Head of State, Bandung, June 7–10, 1979*, Heri Akhmadi. 1981. 201 pp. ISBN 0-87763-001-1.

Number 57   *Permesta: Half a Rebellion*, Barbara S. Harvey. 1977. 174 pp. ISBN 0-87763-003-8.

Number 55   *Report from Banaran: The Story of the Experiences of a Soldier during the War of Independence*, Maj. Gen. T. B. Simatupang. 1972. 186 pp. ISBN 0-87763-005-4.

Translation Series

Language Texts

INDONESIAN

Beginning Indonesian through Self-Instruction, John U. Wolff, Dédé Oetomo, Daniel
    Fietkiewicz. 3rd revised edition 1992. Vol. 1. 115 pp. ISBN 0-87727-529-7. Vol.
    2. 434 pp. ISBN 0-87727-530-0. Vol. 3. 473 pp. ISBN 0-87727-531-9.

Indonesian Readings, John U. Wolff. 1978. 4th printing 1992. 480 pp.
    ISBN 0-87727-517-3

Indonesian Conversations, John U. Wolff. 1978. 3rd printing 1991. 297 pp.
    ISBN 0-87727-516-5

Formal Indonesian, John U. Wolff. 2nd revised edition 1986. 446 pp.
    ISBN 0-87727-515-7

TAGALOG

Pilipino through Self-Instruction, John U. Wolff, Maria Theresa C. Centeno, Der-Hwa
    V. Rau. 1991. Vol. 1. 342 pp. ISBN 0-87727—525-4. Vol. 2. 378 pp. ISBN 0-87727-
    526-2. Vol 3. 431 pp. ISBN 0-87727-527-0. Vol. 4. 306 pp. ISBN 0-87727-528-9.

THAI

A. U. A. Language Center Thai Course, J. Marvin Brown. Originally published by the
    American University Alumni Association Language Center, 1974. Reissued by
    Cornell Southeast Asia Program, 1991, 1992. Book 1. 267 pp. ISBN 0-87727-506-
    8. Book 2. 288 pp. ISBN 0-87727-507-6. Book 3. 247 pp. ISBN 0-87727-508-4.

A. U. A. Language Center Thai Course, Reading and Writing Text (mostly reading), 1979.
    Reissued 1997. 164 pp. ISBN 0-87727-511-4.

A. U. A. Language Center Thai Course, Reading and Writing Workbook (mostly writing),
    1979. Reissued 1997. 99 pp. ISBN 0-87727-512-2.

KHMER

Cambodian System of Writing and Beginning Reader, Franklin E. Huffman. Originally
    published by Yale University Press, 1970. Reissued by Cornell Southeast Asia
    Program, 4th printing 2002. 365 pp. ISBN 0-300-01314-0.

Modern Spoken Cambodian, Franklin E. Huffman, assist. Charan Promchan, Chhom-
    Rak Thong Lambert. Originally published by Yale University Press, 1970.
    Reissued by Cornell Southeast Asia Program, 3rd printing 1991. 451 pp. ISBN
    0-300-01316-7.

Intermediate Cambodian Reader, ed. Franklin E. Huffman, assist. Im Proum. Originally
    published by Yale University Press, 1972. Reissued by Cornell Southeast Asia
    Program, 1988. 499 pp. ISBN 0-300-01552-6.

Cambodian Literary Reader and Glossary, Franklin E. Huffman, Im Proum. Originally
    published by Yale University Press, 1977. Reissued by Cornell Southeast Asia
    Program, 1988. 494 pp. ISBN 0-300-02069-4.

HMONG

White Hmong-English Dictionary, Ernest E. Heimbach. 1969. 8th printing, 2002. 523 pp.
    ISBN 0-87727-075-9.

VIETNAMESE

Intermediate Spoken Vietnamese, Franklin E. Huffman, Tran Trong Hai. 1980. 3rd
    printing 1994. ISBN 0-87727-500-9.

* * *

Southeast Asian Studies: Reorientations. Craig J. Reynolds and Ruth McVey. Frank H. Golay Lectures 2 & 3. 70 pp. ISBN 0-87727-301-4.

Javanese Literature in Surakarta Manuscripts, Nancy K. Florida. Vol. 1, *Introduction and Manuscripts of the Karaton Surakarta.* 1993. 410 pp. Frontispiece, illustrations. Hard cover, ISBN 0-87727-602-1, Paperback, ISBN 0-87727-603-X. Vol. 2, *Manuscripts of the Mangkunagaran Palace.* 2000. 576 pp. Frontispiece, illustrations. Paperback, ISBN 0-87727-604-8.

Sbek Thom: Khmer Shadow Theater. Pech Tum Kravel, trans. Sos Kem, ed. Thavro Phim, Sos Kem, Martin Hatch. 1996. 363 pp., 153 photographs. ISBN 0-87727-620-X.

In the Mirror: Literature and Politics in Siam in the American Era, ed. Benedict R. O'G. Anderson, trans. Benedict R. O'G. Anderson, Ruchira Mendiones. 1985. 2nd printing 1991. 303 pp. Paperback. ISBN 974-210-380-1.

www.ingramcontent.com/pod-product-compliance
Ingram Content Group UK Ltd.
Pitfield, Milton Keynes, MK11 3LW, UK
UKHW012253060225
454777UK00009B/772